A HEART FOR HIS DELIGHTS

Ken Hepner

7710-T Cherry Park Dr, Ste 224
Houston, TX 77095
(713) 766-4271

Cover design by Teresa Granberry, www.HarvestCreek.net

Printed in the United States of America

ISBN: 978-1-0880-2315-0

Dedication

Dedicated to: My wife Raina whom I cherish, my grandmother Sally Hepner, who prayed me into the kingdom, Elsie, Esther, Joyce and Andrea who have prayed for Raina and me for decades!

Table of Contents

Foreword

Alice and I have known and admired Pastor Ken Hepner and his wife Raina since the mid-1990s. They are two of God's finest.

Ken is a pastor's pastor. He has invested his life in leading the churches he's served, but not limited to that. He has a Kingdom vision for the city, state and beyond, and is a mentor to pastors.

This book, "A Heart for His Delights," is a work of love from Ken to us. Inside, you'll immediately see that Ken loves God, and God's kids, and wants to see us positioned to be a blessing to God and to be blessed by God. Both require us knowing God's heart.

Ken wants us to move our focus from what we can get from God, to what we can give to Him. The essence of godliness is found in knowing what pleases the Father and giving it to Him.

Each chapter in this book bursts with revelation like a spiritual kaleidoscope. I encourage you to set aside time each day to take another look.

- **Eddie Smith**, Executive Director, *www.USPrayerCenter.org*

Introduction

There are several things implied in the title of this book, which I want to flesh out as we begin to consider together the things the Lord may want to say to us. First and foremost, this book is written from the perspective of embracing a heart for God and the things that delight the heart of God, what He values, holds as precious, and highly esteems. I am thoroughly captivated by the Biblical teaching on an experience with God that radically changes a person's heart. In the Bible the heart is considered to be absolutely essential in living the Christian life. The heart is seen as the very essence of one's life, the seat of one's affections and decision-making, the place in our lives where the Holy Spirit dwells, and the issue that the Lord God considers first when he looks at our lives.

There is a marvelous story found in the Old Testament that illustrates how the Lord God views the contents of our hearts. When God was issuing the call for the second king of Israel to arise, the one He had chosen to take Saul's place, He told His man Samuel he wasn't looking at the right things when he saw Jesse's son Eliab and thought he was the one. In I Samuel16:7 God says, *"Do not consider his appearance or his height, for I the Lord have rejected him. The Lord does not look at the things man looks at. Man looks at the outward appearance, but the Lord looks at the heart."*

Let's be straight with one another as we begin this journey together discovering the things that God esteems and takes great delight in. We are all involved in a battle for the contents, character, and affections of our hearts! We are all involved in the daily battle to make quality choices of the heart, to espouse godly desires within, and then act in our lifestyle choices in God-honoring ways.

Could we establish together another thing that is open and honest? In our culture here in North America we do not do the heart part of our spirituality well. We tend to serve the Lord with our heads and our deeds, and we tend to think that passionate spirituality is little more than emotionalism for the uneducated. I couldn't disagree with that more strongly than I do! Passion can be emotional but is definitely not emotionalism. Passion is a choice to follow a way of life with yearning and desire to do it well. I think passion of the heart and will is the missing ingredient in North American Christianity. This missing ingredient is why we get all caught up in the stuff of this world system!

In our culture in North America, we are confronted with a set of cultural values based on consumerism, which is the unbridled pursuit of everything we didn't know we needed in order to be happy. This system of values teaches us that true happiness and inner satisfaction is one purchase away. And, of course, the truth is that happiness always remains one purchase away. Consumerism's mantra is "You are what you own or have the ability to buy." Our Christian value is that your worth is based on what you are, not what you possess.

Consumerism is in essence antithetical to what has been true of historic Christianity for two thousand years. Jesus is Lord can't be merely a creed I recite, but rather must be a lifestyle I embrace in every way. Unbridled selfishness is the exact opposite of living a godly, content, and self-controlled lifestyle under His leadership. Paul wrote to his son Timothy, in the context of turning away from loving money, I Timothy 6:6 *"godliness with contentment is great gain."*

God the Spirit desires to live in and transform our hearts, making our lives wellsprings of His life in a parched world. Satan and his minions want to crush and defile our hearts, inciting us to make choices that are based on selfishness and to satisfy our appetites in self-centered, sinful and fleshly, or lustful ways.

King Solomon is the one who wrote the words of this incredible verse: Proverbs 4:23 *"Above all else guard your heart for it is the wellspring of life."* I grieve over the fact that this man who started out so well didn't follow his own advice. He permitted his desires to get completely out of control and lusted for women whom he was commanded by God not to love. The wisest man on the earth at the time died a sensuous old fool whose "heart was led astray by his love of foreign women!" The heart is indeed critical to our spirituality is it not?

Paul prayed for the Ephesian believers to experience the indwelling Holy Spirit in their hearts: *"I pray that out of his glorious riches he may strengthen you with power through his Spirit in your inner being, so that Christ may dwell in your hearts through faith."* Ephesians 3:16, 17a

Romans 5:5 *"And hope does not disappoint us, because God has poured out his love into our hearts by the Holy Spirit, whom he has given us."*

The foundational truth this book asserts is that God has revealed to us in Scripture some things He delights in, cherishes, things He considers precious and highly esteems. We are going to look at passages where He reveals these values to us and seek to make personal applications of those passages in our lives today. We are God's sons and daughters in Christ Jesus. We have been adopted into His family and we bear a new family resemblance: Like Father, like sons and daughters.

Furthermore, embracing Jesus as Savior is inviting Him to be Lord, Master, our King. We become His royal subjects, members of His kingdom of the heart. The sweet thing about knowing Him as our King is that we are given open access into His royal throne room, total access to His presence anywhere and anytime we want to "enter in." In the Old Testament kingdom terms of court protocol, when the King had a special servant/friend who had come to see him, he would raise his scepter to that person and they could ask anything they wanted of him.

It is pictured in Nehemiah and Artaxerxes, Daniel and Nebuchadnezzar, Esther and Xerxes. Similarly the Lord smiles and raises His scepter to me any time I show up to be with Him because I am His cherished servant/friend! That is a truth I hold in my heart of which I hope to never lose sight. The Lord of heaven and earth and all that exists loves me, desires to be with me, and smiles when I enter the courtroom of heaven to invest time with Him daily at 5:30 AM.

I am touched by the thought of what a young Jewish maiden named Hadassah did when she was forced into a "Queen finding contest." Before she was made Queen to Xerxes, Hadassah, who became Queen Esther, was told she would have to invest an entire year immersed in royal beauty treatments. The young Jewish maiden, although inexperienced in the ways of love, understood the fact that the real goal of this year of her life was to please the king. Esther understood a powerful truth that would become foundational for an entire year of her life and would result in a life-altering experience. She understood that her focus was to become beautiful to one set of eyes, to capture the favor of one heart – that of Xerxes.

So she gladly submitted herself to the leadership of a man named Hegai, the lead royal eunuch, who knew everything there was to know about the king. Under the supervision of this man who knew the king intimately, she also would learn to know the delights of the king. Hegai's counsel enabled her to understand what fragrances the king delighted in, the textures and fabrics he liked to touch, and the colors he enjoyed seeing worn by a beautiful woman. She learned about his favorite cosmetics and beauty enhancements. She learned about his favorite foods and drinks, and what the king enjoyed in the company of a beautiful woman. She consumed herself with the thought of engaging the king and bringing him the most pleasure from her companionship with him that she possibly could.

Esther gave herself as completely as she could in the yearlong process of learning the king's delights, not so that she would have knowledge of facts to be able to speak. This was not at all a merely intellectual pursuit. The young Jewish maiden immersed herself completely in those things the king valued by living out what she was learning. And as a result, she won the heart of the king and he made her his queen.

This is an illustration from the natural with tremendous spiritual implications for our lives as God's royal subjects today. In this book I am asking you to ask yourself a critical question. What would my experience with God look like if I invested an entire year of my life immersed in understanding and giving myself to what gives my King Jesus great delight? That is the goal of this book you hold in your hand! Please don't read through it quickly. Take your time and let the truths here immerse your heart in His delights, so that you are making lifestyle choices based on what God delights in.

Your Hegai, so to speak, will be me as I am guided to and attempt to share streams of truth from the Scriptures. Our primary source of knowledge of the ways of our King Jesus is the Word of God, the Bible. I'd like to have your permission to introduce you to themes in the Word of God that serve your spiritual formation around our King's delights much like Hegai formed Hadassah's candidacy for Queen of Persia around Xerxes' delights.

If we know the truth regarding things that the Lord God delights in and esteems we can give ourselves to those things as values in our hearts too. Loving and desiring what delights the Lord God can be a grid we use to embrace some attitudes and behaviors that lead us to be godly, and to turn away from attitudes and behaviors that grieve Him or break His heart. What a simple and yet profound way to cultivate intimacy with our God.

The Lord God has revealed His heart to us in the Scriptures. He loves us with an everlasting love and desires to walk through life with us in a deeply personal and close walk. Jesus came to earth to pay the penalty for our sins and to make it possible for us to be engaged in a personal experience with God by His indwelling Spirit. He purposes to fill us with His Spirit again and again if we simply ask Him to. He purposes to set our hearts on fire with His love, to captivate us and restore to us the joy of His salvation.

Our part in this relationship of love with the Father, Jesus the Son, the Holy Spirit is to cultivate a soft and teachable heart. We each are responsible to be the keepers of our hearts, to tend to what we permit to enter our hearts and live there. Let's be honest with each other and admit that we live in a self-centered and consumer-driven cultural value system. To ask the basic question North American question, "What is in this for me?" is definitively not a kingdom-focused way to live. The road of consumerism is one that absolutely leads in the opposite direction from the kinds of values God has clearly defined for us in Scripture. It is a mere mirage of happiness that never delivers the goods. It is therefore, antithetical to living a Christian – that is Christ-like life and something I must reject if I am to be His follower.

If we choose what delights our King Jesus, we will experience the joy of His renewing presence in our lives every day as the Holy Spirit walks with us and works to transform us into the image of Jesus. We are simply asked to embrace the passion the Lord desires to pour into us, to welcome His will and desires to live in us. The Holy Spirit is a person, and as such, He can be grieved by our lack of desire for Him or welcomed by the invitation we extend to Him to live in our hearts. Where He is welcomed or longed for, He dwells in presence and power. Where He dwells in power He transforms life and where He transforms the life of a person He uses that life to create hunger in other hearts.

I think there are three far better questions to ask than the self-centered, "What's in it for me?" I've been welcoming the church family I have the privilege of walking with to ask these critical kingdom of the heart questions with me. They are:

1. Am I choosing to fix may gaze on Jesus, to behold the Lamb of God who takes away the sin of the world today?
2. Have I embraced John's prayer as the ongoing lifestyle I desire to live: He must increase; I must decrease?
3. Lord Jesus, what are you planning to do in my life and through my life today that I may join you in doing?

I am convinced of the simple truth that everyone who enters into a personal relationship with the Lord Jesus really wants to be a true disciple, but things get in the way of that happening consistently. We generally don't make conscious choices to turn away from God's heart. We tend to simply permit laxity and spiritual slippage to occur over time. Busyness, business, materialism, and other desires can and do sidetrack us. Often what we need is a simple catalyst to call us back to our first love for the Lord Jesus Christ, and we will respond with a ready "yes." I am writing this book with the hope of it being a catalyst for people who will choose to be passionate for God, renewed in spirit, and who will in turn challenge others to be renewed.

As I conclude this introduction section, I want you to know that I am a very simple man, who wants to know and please my King. I am on a journey of the heart just like you are. We are people who need to experience a new move of the Spirit of God in inner transformation and heart cleansing. We need to be called back to our first love, the foundations of brokenness, contrition, repentance of human ways, and hungering passionately for the presence and power of God.

If the Lord has called you to this kind of passion and hunger, you are among a new breed of men and women whom God is raising up in the world to minister in reestablishing foundations of spirituality. A few years ago I sensed the Lord leading me to fast and pray my way through a **personal vision statement**, which would guide my life for my remaining years in ministry with Him. Here's what I sensed the Lord directing me to do: **I am called to help as many as I can as much as I can for as long as I can.** The book you hold in your hand is a simple man's attempt to fulfill what the Lord has asked me to do with Him.

I trust this book will be a spiritual hoot for you as you read it, or at the very least you will discover in the end, you aren't alone, you aren't crazy, and you're in good company!

Written in love for Jesus and my wife Raina …

Ken Hepner

Mifflintown, PA

Chapter One

Circumcision of the Heart

I'd like us to remember the truth that we are all engaged in a significant battle to keep our hearts devoted to knowing God personally and loving God so much that we will choose to do what gives Him great delight. When Solomon wrote in the Proverbs, 4:23 *"Above all else guard your heart for it is the wellspring of life,"* he was giving us a pretty important message about our heart's desires. You and I are the keepers of what we cherish in our hearts. Spiritual passion is essentially embracing a deep desire and longing to know and walk with God. Spiritual passion in my heart is first a choice of my will and then it becomes my motivation and guide to my actions.

Jesus' message was pretty clear when He began His ministry among us. *"Repent for the kingdom of heaven is near you."* This is a clarion call to think in terms of God's Kingdom invading the earth, to think about something that is far bigger than my own life and my little corner of the world. It is as though Jesus was saying straight to my heart, "Ken, because of who I am and what I have come to do for your salvation, the kingdom of God is within your grasp right now. Knowing God intimately Ken, is right at your fingertips so reach out and touch Him."

We all enter the kingdom of God through the very same doorway of voluntary humility, to confess our need of a Savior. We are all called to repent of sin, believe in Christ Jesus' finished work on the cross, that His death pays the penalty of our sin, and receive Him into our hearts as risen Lord Jesus! The gift of salvation by faith in Christ is really the miracle of new birth – there are two people, two personalities, two mentalities, and two sets of desires living in one body. You and I live in our physical body with the Holy Spirit of the Living God.

In the kingdom of God in Christ Jesus there are inherent transcendent truths and values that each adherent is invited to embrace. One of the key values in this kingdom of heaven on earth is that we love both God and people. Loving God first and foremost, with all my heart, soul, mind, will, and body is a call to value what God values that we esteem as precious what God esteems as precious. That means we care for people far more than we value the stuff of this world system, possessions, status, and material things.

As we unpack this concept of inherent and transcendent values I would like you to consider with me that the Bible teaches us a basic truth about living in the blessing of God. If we know the truth and seek to live the truth we will be blessed, that is we will enjoy the smile of God's favor in our lives. The Lord Jesus taught us that if we honored Him with our hearts, our desires, the material possessions we're entrusted with, and if we gave to those who had need we would experience the blessing of God.

For me this whole concept of living under the blessing of the Lord has taken on a brand new theme in my heart in the past seven years. For the past seven years of my life I have lived with the excruciating pain of having blown two discs that have damaged my sciatic nerve. Living with intense pain and suffering, one can't get away from twenty four hours per day for three years, can be an incredible teacher. The same God, who loved me and blessed me when I wasn't in pain, has carried me for the past seven years of walking in pain.

The popular theological position of many people in the church world of North America has placed a definition on the word "blessing" that I can't accept. May I be straight up with you? I know it's a novel concept, but I have a really simple grid that I pass Biblical teaching through, which I have had in my heart for nineteen years. If it isn't true for my friends in southern Africa who struggle to get enough food for their family to eat one descent meal each day, it probably isn't a kingdom ethic.

There are lots of people who are being taught a North Americanism, as a kingdom value. The teaching goes that living under the blessing of God has to do with God wanting all of His children to be happy, with having all the money we need, and the material provisions we desire. For me, and what the Lord has been doing in my heart, that definition is taken from the wrong testament and the wrong covenant. I'd like you to consider with me the vast amount of difference between the definition of the term "blessing" in the Old Covenant with God and the definition of "blessing" in the New Covenant with God.

In the Old Testament how do we know a man is considered to be under the blessing of God? He drives the luxury camel or has the sporty "tricked out" model of the colt, and has a twelve-bedroom, 4500 square foot tent as his home. He had 12 sons, 9 daughters, eight wives, five concubines, had material possessions in great abundance. He owns cattle, sheep, donkeys, camels, and he sits with the elders in a seat of respect at the city gates. In short, his prosperity and public esteem are the proof of his "blessing of God."

In seeming direct contrast in the New Covenant, a person who walks with Jesus is considered to be under the blessing of God not by what he has in terms of this world's goods, but by what he permits to God to remove from his life. In the New Covenant a person is blessed when he goes to the cross and permits God's Son to take things out of his heart and soul, things that are inhibiting his or her walk with the Lord. In the New Covenant a person is blessed by what he gives away to benefit the kingdom of God and not by what he gets and hoards to himself.

In Deuteronomy 30 Moses calls the people to love the Lord their God wholeheartedly, which is the heartbeat of commitment. There is an incredible word to them about what God would do for them in their hearts in response to their choice to love Him. Read with me verse 6:

"The Lord your God will circumcise your hearts and the hearts of your descendents so that you may love him with all your heart and with all your soul and live."

Paul reiterates this incredible word about a circumcised heart in Romans 2:29 *"No, a man is a Jew if he is one inwardly; and circumcision is circumcision of the heart, by the Spirit, not by the written code. Such a man's praise is not from men, but from God."* And in Colossians 2:11, 12 *"In him you were also circumcised, in the putting off of the sinful nature, not with a circumcision done by the hands of men, but with the circumcision done by Christ, having been buried with him in baptism and raised with him through your faith in the power of God, who raised him from the dead."*

Circumcision, in the natural realm, is cutting away something useless in order that the physical body will be bettered. Why does a medical professional circumcise a little boy? He is doing so to increase the sanctity and sensitivity. Why does God say he will circumcise the hearts of his people? **He is telling us He will cut away what is spiritually useless to us in heaven in order to increase the sanctity, the personal holiness we live in and our sensitivity to His voice of direction and leadership in our lives**. Paul's concluding words in Romans 2:29 are that a person who holds still for the cutting work of the Holy Spirit in the heart is a person whose praise is not from men but from God. As a man who wants to be a follower of Jesus that is a pretty important sequence of words to me!

And let's be honest at even deeper levels. Jesus said, "What is highly esteemed among humans is detestable to God." God will cut away the things in our hearts that are crowding out spiritual life and health, things that are valued by the world system in which we live. In this chapter we are talking about embracing the blessing and favor of God. Let's be clear with one another that the Word of God teaches us to value what God values, to keep in step with the Holy Spirit who lives in us. Let's also be clear on the fact that the material blessedness of the North American value system is not a kingdom ethic. God's blessing may include material prosperity and it may not. But one thing is certainly true of materialism as it works its way into my life: It definitely has a desensitizing effect on my heart's pursuit of God's presence!

In John 15 Jesus introduced us to His Father God with the metaphor of a Gardener. He said the gardener, who is good at tending to his vineyards, will take a fruitful branch and prune it back, cut it, so that it will be more fruitful. So it sounds like kingdom fruit bearing requires that we hold still for cutting work!

The Folly of Material Happiness

Proverbs 23:4, 5 *"Do not wear yourself out to get rich; have the wisdom to show restraint. Cast but a glance at riches and they are gone, for they will surely sprout wings and fly off to the sky like an eagle."*

I Timothy 6:6 – 9 *"But godliness with contentment is great gain. For we brought nothing into the world and we can take nothing out of it. But if we have food and clothing, we will be content with that. People who want to get rich fall into temptation and a trap and into many foolish and harmful desires that plunge men into ruin and destruction."*

The first thing we need to do is to examine what the Bible has to say about the insidious creeping allure of consumerism, the insatiable quest for material happiness! The world's value system blares at us with alarming regularity: "If you can just get this better paying job, this thing -- car, house, or recreational activities, you will have found material nirvana and you will be truly happy!"

The philosophical issue behind that statement is that we are ultimately living for the here and now. Consumerism thrives on being driven to achieve true happiness. One doesn't have to actually be rich in the things and goods of this world to have this issue be a really significant inward wrestling match. Paul told Timothy it is a matter of getting our wants and needs mixed up, a matter of the heart's desires. *"People who want to get rich fall into temptation."* The Bible calls us to be the people of God in Christ Jesus, who are called to not live ultimately for the things that this world can supply to us. We're asked to make the choice of the heart to live simply, with a generous and giving heart attitude, in the here and now. There is a huge difference between living for something and living in something!

Peter wrote to the followers of Jesus and encouraged us all to think of ourselves as passing through this world on our way to another destination, and therefore to think of the desires we deal with for the things of this world in light of that truth. I Peter 2:11 *"Dear friends, I urge you, as aliens and strangers in the world, to abstain from sinful desires, which war against your soul."*

The truth is that materialism cannot deliver the goods promised because the fact is that nothing outward will ever bring us to a place of deep inner satisfaction or happiness. Material things were never meant to be cherished in the heart. They were meant for our use, not for our adoration. The Lord Jesus taught us in Matthew 6:19, *"Do not store up for yourselves treasures on earth."* And as He finished that thought He told us why we shouldn't store up treasures for ourselves in the here and now, *"where moth and rust corrupt and where thieves break in and steal."* It wasn't because material things are necessarily evil but that it isn't very smart to put high value on something that doesn't last. The Psalmist says, in Psalm 49:16, 17 *"Do not be overawed when a man grows rich, when the splendor of his house increases; for he will take nothing with him when he dies, his splendor will not descend with him."*

The Choking Affect of Things:

Luke 8:14 *"The seed that fell among thorns stands for those who hear, but as they go on their way they are choked by life's worries, riches and pleasures, and they do not mature."*

I Timothy 6:10 *"For the love of money is a root of all kinds of evil. Some people, eager for money, have wandered from the faith and pierced themselves with many griefs."*

Notice that what Jesus is talking about in the parable of the sower is the choking affect things can have on the ability to know and understand what really matters, the essence of where real life is lived. Notice also in Paul's words to Timothy it isn't necessarily the accumulation of things but the desire to have many things that is at the very root of all kinds of evil.

Let's break this choking affect down into four categories:

Values – the accumulation of material things often has to do with our search for significance. In North American culture, our contemporary society seems to determine status and significance on the basis of income, possessions, and accomplishments. The moniker is: "You are what you have the ability to buy." It seems that if we want to be highly regarded a good income, a great house, a nice wardrobe, the outward appearance of success is a good place to begin. When we permit ourselves to get sucked into the values of materialism and accomplishment, we can miss the truth that there is a completely different and ultimately higher value system in the kingdom of God. Our calling in life as God's people is to love God deeply, love people, and use the things of this world to invest in kingdom ethics.

Time – The accumulation of our stuff is one thing. Taking care of all of our stuff is another thing entirely. The time constraints put on us, by all of the time and labor saving devices we own, is staggering! The value of living simply demands that I take a look at the time constraints my accumulation of things has placed on me. If I am too busy taking care of things to hold my wife's hand and take her for a walk, or roll my grandchildren around on the living room carpet, I am too busy and some things have to go. In the verse cited earlier from Luke 8:19 Jesus said the things of this world can have a choking affect and one of the things they can choke is our time to invest in relationships.

Attention – The accumulation of our stuff has another significant affect on us that we, as followers of Jesus, God's sons and daughters, must think about. The things we have to do in order to get and maintain the material things of this world can and does sap our ability to give attention to other values in life. The accumulation of what we can provide for ourselves also has a net effect of removing us from the immediacy of knowing that we are ultimately dependent on God as our ultimate source of life and peace. Jesus' words are also relevant regarding choking out true life. When having and attaining things in life choke out my ability to understand that I really do need to know and walk with God, I have permitted materialism to grip me!

Debt Load/Worries – For people in North American culture debt load and worries over making ends meet truly affect the pace we live on and the peace we live in. Worries over finance charges, maxing out credit cards, and 120% mortgages are a significant drain on the inner resources of joy in the human heart. If you are in a position to do so, get out of debt as quickly as you possibly can. If you have any credit cards with a 15 % or higher APR get rid of them. Pay them off and cancel them as quickly as you can.

--At the time of this writing there is a tremendously funny commercial on TV about a man named Stanley Johnson who owns everything there is to possibly own, but has gotten it by being "in debt up to his eyeballs." He asks the question at the end of the commercial, "Can anybody help me?" And what makes this so funny is that it's a commercial from a mortgage company to help Stanley to get another loan!

The Lord Jesus Worked to Remove Some Things from Peter's Life:

In Jesus' words to his disciples in Luke 9:23, 24 there is a powerful truth communicated to them and us about allowing Jesus to remove some things from our lives. *"If anyone would come after me he must deny himself and take up his cross daily and follow me. For whoever wants to save his life will lose it, but whoever loses his life for me will save it."*

In order to handle true blessedness, anointing for His kingdom work, and to walk in favor with God and people, Jesus will take some things out of our lives as we fellowship with Him at the cross daily. That is exactly what Jesus did in the life of his friend, the impetuous and brash fisherman named Simon Peter – Rocky!

Can you imagine what Peter's website would have looked like after Pentecost if the Lord hadn't been so hard on his selfishness, sinfulness, and ego issues? I can just see the options on his website now. "Come hear Apostle Peter preach at the Forum!" "Hear the Apostle Peter the author of two of the books of the Bible!" "3000 people were saved in his first sermon!" "Come and see Peter do shadow falling healing ministries!" "Let Peter place his hands on you to impart the new healing anointing into your life."

Jesus worked in Peter's life to cut away sin, which is actually rooted in our self-interest. There are a lot of people in the church who believe that sin is the transgression of a known law, but that is not the essence of sin. The essence of sin is our insidious self-interest! And honestly, consumerism is the ultimate expression of self-interest! Before a law is broken by a bad choice there is a leaning to self in the heart, the disease of self-interest. Jesus wants to cut that out of all of His followers, and he did so in Peter's life. At his calling and the miraculous catch of fish when Jesus had him put out into the deep for a catch and they took in an enormous catch, Peter is led to see his own self-interest and sin in his soul and cries out, "Go away from me Lord, for I am a sinful man."

Jesus worked in Peter's life to cut away the presence of selfishness. On the mount of transfiguration Peter wanted to build shelters for them all so he could hang out with Jesus, Moses, and Elijah. What a selfish thing to think, let alone to say in the context of an appearance of God Almighty with His One and Only Son. Lord, let's stay here forever! Let the other nine disciples and the rest of the people fend for themselves because I am having a ball. When Jesus talked about being crucified and raised from the dead, Peter's initial response was to take the Lord aside and confront him with his perspective that this couldn't happen. Jesus was concerned about what this would mean in the future ministry of His apostle. This had to be cut out of Peter's heart and Jesus was pretty confrontational with him.

The last thing Jesus cut out of Peter's life, preparing him for sacred use, and to be vessel of honor, and a man who could correctly handle and seek to manifest the glory of God on the earth, was his bullish self-reliance. In the Garden near the Mount of Olives, Matthew 26:31 – 36, Jesus was getting ready to die for us all and predicts their betrayal and scattering. Peter made two rash statements, promises to Jesus that have self-reliance at their core.

Matthew 26:33 *"Peter replied, 'Even if all fall away on account of you, I never will.'"*

Matthew 26:35 *"But Peter declared, 'Even if I have to die with you, I will never disown you.'"*

Just a few hours later, outside of the palace Peter has just denied that he even knows the Lord for the third time and has heard a rooster crow in the distance. Matthew 26:75 *"Then Peter remembered the word*

Jesus had spoken: 'Before the rooster crows, you will disown me three times.' And he went outside and wept bitterly."

In order for Peter to be a vessel of Jesus' honor he had to experience the pain of circumcision of the heart. He had to hold still for the cutting rebuke of Jesus, while He systematically worked to take things that were useless out of Peter's heart and life, so that he could be cleansed and set apart for sacred use.

What is highly esteemed among men is detestable to God. People love the strong and confident leader. What the Lord longs for but doesn't have much of is broken human strength so His strength can be embraced. Peter found this to be true in his own soul, that what Jesus really wanted for his life was brokenness and for him to be empty of self-reliance. The clearly visible fruit of broken human strength is weeping, godly sorrow that leads to repentance! The tears he cried that night of Jesus' death were an "Aha experience" Peter would never forget. Some things had to be cut out of his heart to make him ready to walk in the blessing and the anointing of the Holy Spirit's power flowing through him!

Circumcision of the heart is definitely not something that we hear a lot of teaching about these days in the church and over the airways of radio and TV preaching. What we seem to hear a good bit is that God wants to make you happy and wants you to have a really good life right now. My response to that humanly focused teaching is to ask a bigger question. The question that comes to me is: What is the good life right now? The truth is that God wants to enable us to walk in his blessing in our lives and in order for him to give us true spiritual riches he will walk us through really painful circumstances and cut some things out of us that prevent us from embracing the things that are truly blessings.

After many years of walking with Jesus, knowing the joy of being used by God to preach and to help people, I still see things in my heart that I don't like very much. Recently, the Lord has been walking me through a time of soul-searching and has shown me places of self-interest and self-reliance that dwell in my heart. He has me at a place of heart circumcision, of brokenness and repentance, and to be honest with you, while it certainly isn't pleasant for me, I am humbled and grateful that God loves me so deeply that He has chosen to show me what He wants to remove from me.

Investing My Life in Spiritual Riches

Matthew 13:44 – 46 *"The kingdom of heaven is like treasure hidden in a field. When a man found it, he hid it again, and then went and sold all he had and bought the field. Again, the kingdom of heaven is like a merchant looking for fine pearls. When he saw one of great value, he went away and sold everything he had and bought it."*

I have heard it said that the person who did this, found the treasure, hid it again and then bought the field so he could rightfully own the treasure, was acting deceptively and was only out for material gain. The logic is OK but it misses the whole point of the parable, which by the way is a story that is told in order to make a broader point. The point here is that there is greater treasure than what can be experienced in the material world and that treasure is attainable if we simply go after it with our whole heart.

And as a point of information this is not necessarily a true story taken from the Jerusalem Post Gazette, because everyone knows that everything one reads in the newspaper is completely accurate. The whole point of this story is the existence of true treasure, that we can get beyond human treasure and know the truth that there is something that really does satisfy the inner heart-cry we all have. There is in all of our lives a sense of nagging incompleteness, an inner discontent that only finds its satisfaction in knowing God as our Father in a personal way.

What Jesus is saying is that He is the Pearl of Great Price and He is the Treasure hidden in a field. As we come to know Him as Savior and walk in an intimate relationship with God by faith in Him, that relationship is true treasure. There are riches in the kingdom of heaven that are much greater and make us much richer than money or possessions ever could. Read the following Scriptures to see what the Bible says about true riches and living much more simply:

II Corinthians 4:7 *"But we have this treasure in jars of clay to show that the all-surpassing power is from God and not from us."*

Ephesians 1:7 *"In him we have redemption through his blood, the forgiveness of sins, in accordance with the riches of God's grace."*

Ephesians 2:7 *"in order that in the coming ages he might show the incomparable riches of his grace, expressed in his kindness to us in Christ Jesus."*

Ephesians 3:8 *"Although I am less than the least of God's people, this grace was given to me; to preach to the Gentiles the unsearchable riches of Christ."*

Philippians 4:19 *"And my God will meet all your needs according to his glorious riches in Christ Jesus."*

So do you find yourself at a place in life that is difficult for you? Are you walking in a place that is characterized by hard circumstances, a place where the Lord is showing you things in your heart that shouldn't be there? Welcome to the school of God. Heart circumcision is the place the Lord Jesus takes every one of His choice and beloved sons and daughters, to cut out of our hearts what is preventing us from knowing Him more intimately!

We began this look at heart circumcision with the words of Moses in Deuteronomy 30. Dr Eugene Peterson has a unique way with words in his translation of the Bible in The Message. Deuteronomy 30 is a powerful call to love the Lord supremely, to obey the Lord with heartfelt fervor. In that context Dr Peterson quotes Moses writing about this incredible thing that God cuts things out of the hearts of His chosen, treasured people.

> *"God, your God, will cut away the thick calluses on your heart and your children's hearts, freeing you to love God, your God, with your whole heart and soul and live, really live. ...And you will make a new start, listening obediently to God, keeping all his commandments that I'm commanding you today. God, your God, will outdo himself in making things go well for you:"* The Message Version

I love what he says there. Calluses are thick, hardened skin that is much more insensitive, not as responsive as our skin is. Calluses in our hearts would be something that prevent us from feeling and sensing the leadership of the Holy Spirit, from being able to freely respond to His Word and His leading. Thick and hard places of my heart have to be cut away. God will do it if I will hold still for it.

Desert Places – Pain and Suffering

Every person God has used mightily has had a desert experience to live with. You show me the hero of the faith and I will show you a place where God permitted difficulty and pain to cut away the useless from his or her heart. Alone with God in the desert places of life, places of pain and heartache, we are forced to trust Him at deeper levels, to hunger and thirst for His presence to sustain us.

It seems to me that God is interested in revealing the glory of His Son Jesus on the earth, of pouring true treasure into human vessels like you and me. We can't be full of ego and full of the Spirit of Jesus. That can't work. He has to prepare the vessels in order to be able to possess the treasure. Paul's words in II Corinthians 4:7 come to mind, *"We have this treasure in jars of clay to show that this all-surpassing glory is from God and not from us."*

Permit me to leave you with one last insight regarding the surgery the Spirit of God performs in cutting away the useless from our hearts. Have you ever considered the one big difference between King David and his son King Solomon? It is the presence of a wilderness place of suffering in David's life, which Solomon did not have.

David was soft and had developed "a heart after God's own heart" because he had a cave of Adullam experience of suffering in the wilderness at the hands of Saul. For seven years David held still in the desert experience as God shaped him in the school of suffering. As a result, even when he sinned greatly, he repented greatly and was chosen and used by God for generations.

Solomon had no such place of suffering and pain, where God used personal suffering to cut things out of him. When he suffered he chose to be hardened instead of soft and broken hearted like his dad! The wisest man on earth died a sensuous old fool whose heart was led astray by his love of foreign wives.

My brother and sister, this is my Hegai counsel to you as we conclude this chapter. If your heart is broken and you hurt as you see things in your life that shouldn't be there, you are in a wonderful place of inner transformation. Hold still and permit the Spirit of God to cut things out. He cuts away the things from our hearts that will be useless to us in heaven, in order to increase our sanctity our lives and to increase our sensitivity to His voice of leadership and direction. And just as a word of encouragement: He obviously loves you dearly, and plans to use you in ministry to others, if He has taken you into the desert to be with Him in the School of God! Hold still. He isn't finished with you yet! Drink in the truth of Song of Songs 8:5 ***"Who is this coming up out of the desert leaning on her lover?"***

God delights in sons and daughters who have chosen a lifestyle that hungers and thirsts to know Him more intimately than we presently do. Let's hold still while He cuts away that which is keeping us from our desire to know Him more!

Chapter Two

Brokenness and Contrition

I hope you are sensing the truth that this could be a really important journey we take together as we study the Scriptures around the theme of embracing a heart for what God esteems. As the adopted sons and daughters of God, we have been given the incredible privilege of His Spirit's presence in our lives. The King we adore lives in each one of our hearts. We are talking about the things we are called to value and cherish in our hearts as partakers of His nature and adherents to His kingdom.

We live in a "world system" in North America, which has values, standards of morality, and codes of ethics that are quite often in direct conflict with the values of the Kingdom of heaven. Our culture places value on things that are visible and material. Our cultural values are status and social esteem, largely manifested by people who are "successful" in what they do for a living. We value consumerism, the material, the right house in the right neighborhood, the right style of clothes with the right manufacturer's label. Marrying the right spouse with the right look – no cellulite please – will make one happy and increase one's esteem. And of course, if one drives a Lexus or a Benz one has more social status than he who drives a Chevy. You are what you can afford to buy!

When we have been given eternal life in Christ Jesus, we have entered the Kingdom of heaven right here and now on planet earth. As subjects of this new King and Lord it is wise to find out from His revealed Word what makes this King happy and what things bring joy and delight to His heart. We need to remember that our democratically conditioned ears and lifestyle of individual rights and freedoms do not fit well with the issues relative to obeying a King. As partakers of His Kingdom, we need to remember that in the presence of a King what He asks we give, what He tells we do, and where He sends we go. Love for this King and gratitude for our gift of eternal salvation move us to obedience.

One of the primary New Testament metaphors Jesus used to describe how the Kingdom of God impacts the heart of a person is the picture of it being like a marriage. He compares Himself to a bridegroom and us to a bride. What do spouses do as they learn to relate to one another in love? Assuming they aren't too ornery, they try not to do things that bug their spouse and seek to do those things that bring joy and delight to their spouse! As I am writing this book I am walking in my thirty-fourth year of marriage to my sweetheart Raina. One of my great joys in life is to do things that make her happy, that make life more pleasurable for her. To be quite honest with you, I think about ways to do what I know will bring her joy. I never think about pleasing Raina from a "dutiful" or "obligatory" perspective. My motivation is to demonstrate my love to her. I am deeply in love with her, so doing what will make her smile makes me happy.

This is the analogy I have in my heart as we unfold this theme together. We are asking and seeking to find Biblical answers to this question: What are the things that are precious to God Almighty my Lord and King? If I know what is important to Him, I'll know some things I can do to make His heart smile and cause Him joy.

In this chapter we're looking together at the first thing that is precious to the heart of God our Father, Christ Jesus our Master: When we embrace a **Broken and Contrite Heart before Him.** This heart attitude of brokenness, contrition, and voluntary humility is definitely met by God with joy and a smile of loving approval.

Psalm 51:17 *"The sacrifices of God are a broken spirit; a broken and contrite heart, O God, you will not despise."*

Isaiah 57:15 *"For this is what the high and lofty one says – He who lives forever, whose name is holy: I live in a high and holy place, but also with him who is contrite and lowly in spirit, to revive the spirit of the lowly and to revive the heart of the contrite"*.

Isaiah 66:1, 2 *"This is what the Lord says: Heaven is my throne, and the earth is my footstool. Where is the house you will build for me? Where will my resting place be? Has not my hand made all these things, and so they came into being? declares the Lord. This is the one I esteem: he who is humble and contrite in spirit, and trembles at my word"*.

Psalm 34:18 *"The Lord is close to the broken hearted and saves those who are crushed in spirit"*.

When we speak of being brokenhearted and contrite before God we're talking about a heart attitude that God considers to be precious and highly esteemed. We're talking about choosing to have a heart attitude that agrees with God's viewpoint of what we've done wrong or the right things we should have done that we've omitted. We're talking about a heart attitude that feels the emotional and spiritual pain of our having offended God in action or omission, allowing that private pain to break our hearts and move us to deep repentance and change from within.

But there is something deeper here as well. A broken and contrite heart is really a way of life, a voluntary choice to humble our selves before the Lord that He may lift us up. The truth is that we can't live a Christian life that pleases God and is a blessing to us apart from His presence living in us, transforming us into His image. Jesus said it well in John 15:5, "I am the vine; you are the branches. If a man remains in me and I in him, he will bear much fruit; apart from me you can do nothing." As God's children, when we learn the blessed truth that humbling ourselves, being broken hearted and contrite are a way of life that God delights to see in us, spiritual growth, bearing fruit for the kingdom of God, and life-change will be happening in us by His Spirit's transforming power!

We began this chapter by looking at the fact that kingdom values are generally speaking the antithesis of culture's values. This is certainly a case in point. Culture doesn't esteem a soft and broken, contrite heart. The value is rugged individualism; "I don't need anybody or anything to make it in life." There is an enemy to embracing deep brokenness and contrition in our hearts; our human pride we all have to deal with. There is also a fruit of pride that feeds off of our cultural value of rugged individualism; the "I don't need anybody" attitude of pride. The fruit I am speaking of is focusing life on doing our best religious activity, working to try to show God, myself, and others that my efforts for God are what really matter.

There are some really clear things that demonstrate how vastly different an attitude that has essentially chosen to rely on one's own religious efforts is from embracing one's need and following Jesus:

1) Religion focuses on people's efforts to get to God . . . the Christian life is God coming and finding us.

2) Religion satisfies a person's mind with doctrinal dogma . . . a relationship with Jesus Christ as Lord satisfies the longing of our soul.

3) Religion is a person working hard for God . . . the Christian life is about God doing His work in the heart of the person.

4) Religion causes people to do things they really don't want to do but feel guilty if they omit them, things like going to church, or serving the needy, or acts of kindness . . . Christianity causes a person to love what they used to dislike because their hearts are radically changed.

5) <u>Religion</u> focuses on people trying to look good in the eyes of people . . . Christianity makes us look beautiful to God!

6) <u>Religion</u> focuses on the person's pleasure with their own performance . . . Christianity causes us to find pleasure with God and to never quite be pleased with ourselves.

7) <u>Religion</u> focuses on comparing ourselves with other people and concluding that we're good people who God is blessed to have . . . Christianity compares itself with Christ and moves a person to enter a lifelong pursuit of being made to like Him from the heart!

8) <u>Religion</u> works for the accolades of men and rewards that are seen now . . . Christianity longs to please Christ Jesus and lays up treasure in heaven to be laid at His feet.

9) <u>Religion</u> causes us to give away $5000.00 we don't need that we'll write off as a tax deduction anyway . . . Christianity causes us to give away $500.00 we don't really have to spare, believing God wants us to meet a need and delights in our obedience.

God delights in a heart attitude of brokenness and contrition that moves us to be deeply repentant people who long after His heart and His righteousness in our daily lives. It naturally follows that if these attitudes are highly esteemed in God's eyes, our enemy Satan will work to produce resistance to or some kind of pseudo-experience designed to undermine these attitudes living in our hearts.

In order to help us to unpack this truth a bit better there is a wonderful story of the contrast between a life that is focused on religious effort and a life that is broken and contrite before the Lord. It is found in Luke's gospel chapter seven, verses 36 through 50. This is a powerful picture from an everyday life experience Jesus had with two people who were the essence of the message.

Simon the Pharisee: Religious Life

The first thing I'd like to point out about Simon the Pharisee's very religious life was that he is typical of all people who are religious without a relationship with Jesus Christ. Simon had the form of right believing, he could give the right answers, but he had the heart part wrong. He did not exhibit the right character and he had the practical life part in his mind wrong too. Because he had the heart part wrong his thinking was really messed up too.

In his mind he saw Jesus as a very holy man and a great teacher, which was right on the mark but then he made a grave mistake made by many religious people. He assumed that a truly holy prophet would never associate with a person with a sinful reputation. *"If this man were really a prophet, he would know who is touching him and what kind of woman she is – that she is a sinner."*

Simon's view of the Christ was faulty in that he saw the Savior as only a political, pro-Jewish monarch who would redeem Israel from bondage to Rome and would be so holy as to never go near a sinner. When in reality, the Holy One came to be the Merciful One to bring redemption to those of us who desperately needed forgiveness because our sins were so many and were dragging us to hell.

Simon's form of believing was right. It is true that God wants us to live holy lives but in his practical application of his life he was miles from the truth. True holy living is not utter separation from those who are brokenhearted in life and who have sinned. True holiness is an instrument of redemption in the midst of sin; it does not partake of uncleanness but it most certainly reaches to the unclean heart.

This religious and smug attitude in his Pharisaical heart also led Simon to a rather gross misperception of the woman who was so broken in heart, as well.

"If this man were a prophet he would know who is touching him and what kind of woman she is – that she is a sinner."

He was so caught up with his religious traditional teaching and his smug black and white answers based on self-righteousness, that he could not see her obvious signs of having become a repentant, forgiven sinner. He made the awful mistake of holding someone's past sins against them after God had forgiven her and cancelled her debt. Her tears and loving devotion to Jesus point us to the fact that the Lord had done something in her for which she was deeply grateful.

She was obviously unwelcome in his house, let alone kneeling at his feet or touching him and in this attitude he had totally missed what God really wanted him to be about.

Another major truth emerges about religious lives from this man named Simon the Pharisee. He was so wrapped up in himself and how he was perceived, sitting there at the head of the table, that he was blind to and inconsiderate of other's needs. Notice with me that there are three contrasts Jesus uses to show Simon that he was so full of himself that he had failed to give Jesus the most common courteous treatments expected of a good host:

   a. "I came into your house. You did not give me any water for my feet, but she wet my feet with her tears and wiped them with her hair".

   b. "You did not give me a kiss (on the cheek) but this woman, from the time I entered, has not stopped kissing my feet".

   c. "You did not put oil on my head, but she has poured perfume on my feet".

In short Simon, you are so wrapped up in your self-righteousness, in your self-sufficiency and in your self-love you are only able to make sure you look good there at the head of the table while this woman on the other hand has been content to be at my feet. And Simon the moral of the story is you are so full of religious bigotry that you do not see yourself in need of the mercy and forgiveness of God therefore you love God little in your much love of yourself!

My brother or sister, a religiously motivated, hard-hearted person has a big problem before God. He/she is guilty of the sin of self-sufficiency and self-righteousness and you can always recognize a religious life by its fruit:

It is different on Sundays and in front of people than it is in its home or when all alone and nobody else can see how he acts or know what we are thinking. May I remind you that God is Omniscient meaning that He knows everything we do and He will hand out retribution based on how we lived our lives on judgment day?

A life based on religious activity is so concerned with how it looks that it is not moved with love to meet another person's needs. When it does help someone else it makes sure that lots of people are taking notice of its generosity.

A life based on religious activity retains people's sins against them and is very reluctant to believe a person truly is new in Christ Jesus. It calls up all the old junk of the other's life with the aim of belittling or putting down to make itself look better.

The Woman: Salvation

The second character of the story I want us to look at is this precious woman who was so obviously loved deeply by the Lord Jesus because she has experienced a broken heart and has been made utterly new on the inside which worked its way out in her practical living.

I believe this woman came into Simon's house having repented of her sins previously at another place and had received a brand new start from the Lord Jesus. His word of deliverance had touched her life and she came to demonstrate her deep love and devotion to Him for what had already taken place in her heart and soul:

First, notice the sequence of events with me. The Kingdom of Jesus Christ in our hearts, our response of love does not bring His forgiveness. On the contrary He reaches into our lives in forgiveness, cleansing, and renewal and then we are set free to truly love. Jesus is therefore, showing us that her tears that flowed demonstrated her love. Her heart desire to express her loving devotion was a fruit of her repentance and brand new heart!

Secondly, verse 47 places the forgiveness before the love *"her many sins have been forgiven . . . she loves much. But he who has been forgiven little loves little."*

I declare to you emphatically that this dear woman's life preaches loudly and clearly to our lives today in three magnificent ways -

First there is full and free forgiveness for the worst of sinners. Jesus Christ my Savior makes it very clear that He fully understood the depths of her sins and by His actions and His language He reached out to her right where she was at her point of deep need.

Second her heart was broken, she knew she was sinner, she humbled herself and in that act of brokenness our Lord Jesus reached to her and He gave her a fresh start in life *"Your many sins now stand forgiven."*

Third her love as a fruit of her newness in Him was displayed in the most humble and beautiful of ways. She lay at His feet, a vantage point from which it's pretty hard to view yourself as important. At another's feet you are showing that person's importance to you. She kissed His feet, which was an act of sincere adoration and gratitude. She poured expensive perfume on His feet indicating that no gift no matter how costly was too good for her Savior.

The lessons this dear woman's life speaks must be applied to our living, our everyday decision-making as followers of Jesus. In fact, unless we apply the Word to our lives once we've seen what it is speaking there is no experience of the life-altering power of God. They are only Words until they are applied to our heart's desires and worked out in our everyday life choices!

> Am I walking through life with a humble and contrite heart?

> Has my heart been broken, forgiven, and renewed?

> Am I living a life of love to Jesus out of gratitude for what He has done for me?

The Words of Jesus

To my mind's eye the words of Jesus in this text to the two people, are timeless and eternal words of judgment upon the intents and attitudes of the heart. Jesus Christ is consistent yesterday, today, and forever. To the one who sees no need of any repentance like Simon the Pharisee, the words He speaks to the man typify what all religious and self-righteous people will hear: *"He who has been forgiven little, loves little."* Let's be clear with one another folks: This is not a compliment to the self-righteous Pharisee. This is a word of indictment.

The one who sees himself as pretty good and does not need much forgiveness is one who will stand unforgiven and he in turn will love little because he is unforgiven. Jesus was saying a word to Simon the Pharisee that was the beginning of a clear denunciation to religious people of self-righteous attitudes which culminates in the seven, *"Woe to you Scribes, Pharisees, hypocrites!"* statements found in the twenty-third chapter of Matthew.

But Jesus gave three beautiful, tender statements to the penitent woman who had been very sinful.

"Therefore her many sins have been forgiven – for she has loved much."

"Your sins are forgiven".

"Your faith has saved you; go in peace".

Like this woman, when you and I come to Jesus with our hearts broken of our sin, self-interest, and self-reliance, and ask Him for His transforming work in our hearts, we will receive the precious provisions He died to make available to us. A broken and contrite heart in you and me as a way of life is precious to God, highly esteemed, cherished and valued. I love John's words to the brokenhearted in I John 1:9, *"If we confess our sins he is faithful and just and will forgive us of our sins and purify us of all unrighteousness."*

He will cleanse our hearts of everything we have ever done wrong. We will be completely forgiven. Having cleaned our hearts He gives us a brand new start in life with a clean slate to live for Him. Then, the miracle of the new birth, the Holy Spirit creates a new heart, a new set of desires in our lives. Our lives will reflect the newness we have received in genuine love for our Lord and Savior. This act of God on our behalf will set us free to be motivated to love and serve Him with gladness of heart, because complete forgiveness loves the Lord much!

This dear woman's life preaches a great message to us all: God considers very precious, highly esteems brokenness and contrition of heart! This is something we can all embrace and welcome as we seek to draw nearer to God personally. So my Hegai question for you is: Are you choosing to walk through life with a heart attitude characterized by what God esteems, a broken and contrite heart? A heart of love for God is a demonstration of the Holy Spirit's work in us, transformation of the heart. That awesome Biblical truth is available to all of us who believe!

Chapter Three

His Promises

In this chapter we are looking at another thing that God esteems, values, considers precious: His promises He has given to us in the Scriptures. Remember our crucial question we are asking together, the foundation of our study. What does our Lord delight in, esteem as precious, of inestimable valuable? Like Queen Esther modeled for us in her choice to delight her human king, we can give ourselves to that which we know brings delight to our King Jesus.

If we understand from God's revealed Word what He holds as precious and we are His royal subjects we will know what we are called to value in our hearts. And further, if we know what is precious to God we will also have a fundamental understanding of things we can do to please Him, make our King's heart rejoice and bring Him great delight. And, at even deeper levels for our thinking, His delight becomes a grid we can use to say no to things that tempt and entice us to embrace what breaks His heart.

We've also noted a rather basic understanding of what it means to be the people of God, members of His Kingdom here on earth. We have been made part of His holy kingdom of the heart, which places us squarely in opposition to the attitudes, ways, and values of this world system we live in. The Scriptures talk about our "not loving the world" – meaning the system of life you find yourself in that is a combination of the thinking of sinful, the depraved thinking of people, and the wiles of Satan who is "prince of this world." The Bible calls us to love God, one another as Christians, and the lost people of our created world and it calls us to reject loving or embracing the world system or cultural values.

John 14:18, 19 Jesus said, *"If the world hates you, keep in mind that it hated me first. If you belonged to the world it would love you as its own. As it is, you do not belong to the world, but I have chosen you out of the world. That is why the world hates you"*.

I John 2:15 – 17 John taught us as adherents to Jesus' Kingdom here on earth: *"Do not love the world. If anyone loves the world, the love of the Father is not in him. For everything in the world – the cravings of sinful man, the lust of his eyes and the boasting of what he has and does – comes not from the Father but from the world. The world and its desires pass away, but the man who does the will of God lives forever."*

As followers of Jesus Christ, we must make decisions on an ongoing basis to embrace the values of His kingdom, God's good, pleasing, and perfect will. These decisions lead us to reject the values of our world system. This system plays to our sinful, fleshly nature to entice us away from God's ways. We must realize this warfare of values we are in and be willing to pass our attitudes, actions, and lifestyle under the scrutiny of the question, "am I embracing what is precious to you here Father God? Am I embracing your Kingdom values here or the ways of my world culture?"

The people of God in Christ Jesus who are walking in the light of His Kingdom values here on planet earth have chosen to take into consideration that we are living a counter-culture lifestyle. Further, we are learning what it means to pray in the garden of our own souls with Jesus – "it doesn't matter to me Father what I want here, as much as it matters to me what you want here." *"Not my will but your will be done, Father."*

As we delve into the Scriptures together, we are studying another thing that is very precious to God. The Lord considers to be very precious, of great value, His words of promise to be faithful to us in. II Peter 1:4 *"His very great and precious promises, so that through them you may participate in the divine nature and escape the corruption in the world caused by evil desires."* When you and I take seriously the promises He has made to us, appropriate them by faith, and believe Him to fulfill what He has said He will do, He takes great delight in us as His sons and daughters.

In the Bible we have been given the Word of God, the truth as it has been revealed to us in our Lord Jesus Christ. The Word of God is true, because behind it stands the Lord God Almighty who is righteous, just, faithful, and true. Jesus told us He is the way and the truth and the life, and no one comes to the Father except through Him. Jesus can make the claim to be the truth because He is the revelation of God's nature to humanity. If we have truly seen Him we have seen the Father.

By way of contrast, the value of the world system we live in is relativism, which means that there is no such thing as absolute truth, no standard of right and wrong, and "what's true for you might not be true for me." Truth is relative, meaning it's up for grabs, depending on what one desires or chooses. When truth is subjective and relativism rules there is no way to judge whether or not something is untrue, and there are no measurements for us to weigh our attitudes and behaviors.

Relativism's chief aim is to get us to cast doubt on the truth and veracity of the nature of God as it is revealed to us in Scripture. I wonder who is behind that line of reason? Somewhere I read about some serpent in a garden asking a woman, "Did God really say?" Relativism ends with thinking up new ideas of new and special knowledge taken from erroneous "lost books of the Bible" with names like The Gospel of Judas, The Gospel of Peter, The Gospel of Thomas, and the Gospel of Mary Magdalene. Each of these spurious works was shown to be erroneous nearly 1700 years ago. Maybe Jesus wasn't God's Son. Maybe he was simply conceived by a man and woman. Maybe he was married to Mary Magdalene and had children whose descendents are living in the south of France.

We do have a standard of right and wrong. We do have a moral code drawn up and written for us by holy people of old, who were moved and inspired to write it by the Holy Spirit. Morality grows out of its anchor in God's character as a Holy and loving God. Jesus said He is the embodiment of truth itself because He is the revelation of God's character.

The Lord God has given us many promises in His Word concerning His desire to bless us and do great things in our lives. It brings great joy to His heart when we believe those promises so strongly that we'll bring them before His throne, pray them out to Him, and wait for Him to fulfill them. In this passage in Peter's letter, the promises of Jesus to His people are narrowly focused and sharply defined by the context of truth contained in the paragraph. Peter's focus here is to teach us that as people in His Kingdom we have been given His great and precious promises to live on and believe in so strongly that our lives will bear a resemblance to the King, our Lord Jesus, whom we serve; there'll be a family resemblance! The principle is: Like father like sons and daughters.

Jesus is the Guarantor of the Promises

II Peter 1:3 *"His divine power has given us everything we need for life and godliness through our knowledge of Him who called us by His own glory and goodness."*

Please notice with me that it is the person of our Lord and King, Jesus Christ that Peter points us to as the giver and the guarantor of the promises of God, which are so precious. Jesus came to His disciples and called them to be His followers. He promised them that He had come, John 10:10, *"that you might have life and have it more abundantly."* The one who calls them to follow Him also enables and equips them. The one who calls us to follow Him as King, enables and equips us to be His people.

Please also notice with me that it does not say we get everything we want because sometimes our wants may be in conflict with what we really need. Peter says, *"His divine power has given us everything we need for life and godliness."* In Jesus Himself reside two great things:

One – Divine Power, which cannot ultimately be defeated or frustrated. By its very nature it is destined to win in the end. Jesus' love is always backed by His power. Therefore, it is ultimately victorious love. What God says His love will do, in reaching to us and to bless us, will be done!

Two – Divine Generosity – He bestows on us all we need for life in Him and godly living right now. Not only does Jesus teach us what kind of life we ought to live but generously lavishes on us the provisions to live as He asks! He gives us a life that is not a withdrawal from this life but a triumphant involvement in it.

His goal for sharing that is to help us to grasp the awesome grandeur of our King Jesus. All of our provisions are wrapped up in His awesome Person so by getting to know the Giver more and more intimately we get to know more of His gifts. By getting to know Him more intimately as He who promised the power to live a godly life, the more precious are the promises He gave to give us victory in our quest for a godly life!

Peter goes on in that verse to give us two quick glimpses into Jesus' attraction to people. Why is it we are so drawn to this Christ Jesus 2000 years later? What is it about Him that places in our hearts a want to crown Him Lord and King? Peter, as an eyewitness and a disciple, Jesus' deeply surrendered follower, gives us 2 glimpses at Jesus:

Peter says by His "areta" - translated goodness, maybe could be better rendered "moral excellence or virtuousness," thus more loosely "holiness." Perhaps Peter recalled, as he penned these words about Jesus, the time he was out fishing on the Sea of Galilee all night, hadn't caught a thing, and Jesus used his fishing boat as a pulpit. No doubt the words of this holy, kind, compassionate man were like spiritual bombs going off in Peter's heart and soul. Jesus told him to put out into the lake and let down his nets for a huge catch. Reluctantly he obeyed and caught so many fish his boat began to sink and he had to signal another boat to come and help tow the catch.

When it was all over the teaching of this virtuous, kind, compassionate man accompanied by this striking miracle was more than Peter could bear. He fell to the ground on his knees and cried, *"Go away from me Lord I am a sinful man"! Jesus replied, "Don't be afraid Simon; from now on you will catch men."* Have you and I been similarly touched in heart by the beauty and virtue of our King Jesus?

Peter says by His "doxa" - translated glory, dazzling splendor, awesome grandeur. Almost certainly Peter had in mind the Mount of Transfiguration as he wrote about the splendor and glory of Jesus, how he was just shattered inside as he saw the true nature of Jesus that seemed to illuminate the very ground Peter stood on. Peter wasn't merely overwhelmed by the transfiguration of Jesus. It was more Jesus' life and heart revealed to Peter before they arrived at the mountain. Peter's running mate John put it this way in John 1:14 *"And we beheld His glory, the glory as of the only Begotten Son of the Father"*.

Peter uses these two words, glory and goodness, to talk about our Master and King Jesus. He's trying to help us to see that we're bidden to Jesus, drawn to Him on the basis of who He is and the more we intimately know Him the Giver and Guarantor of the promises of God the more precious we'll hold His promises!

Jesus' Promises are for Now

II Peter 1:4a *"Through these He has given us His very great and precious promises so that through them you may participate . . ."*

Peter moves on to tell us a truth we need to have firmly implanted in our hearts. The promises of Jesus Christ our Lord are given to us that our present everyday living will be constantly and profoundly impacted and transformed. It has been left to us to be impacted in the heart here and now with the presence and power of the Spirit of Christ in our daily lives, so that we might be experiencing His glory and goodness and be sharing His glory and goodness in lifestyle and word with other people.

Think about some of His precious promises with me. We don't have to wait until we get to heaven and see Him face to face in order to see and experience and share His glory and goodness. Thanks to His Spirit you and I may participate now in His promises for life and godliness.

FORGIVENESS OF SINS – I John 1:9 *"If we confess our sins he is faithful and just and will forgive us of sin and cleanse us of all unrighteousness."*

ANSWERS TO PRAYER – Mark 11:24 *"Therefore I tell you, whatever you ask for in prayer, believe that you have received it, and it will be yours."*

John 15:7 *"If you remain in me and my words remain in you, ask whatever you wish, and it will be given you."*

THE PRESENCE OF HIS SPIRIT – Luke 11:13 *"If you then, though you are evil, know how to give good gifts to your children, how much more will your Father in heaven give the Holy Spirit to them that ask him!"*

John 14:15, 16 *"If you love me, you will obey my command. And I will ask the Father and He will give you another Counselor to be with you forever – The Spirit of Truth."*

DIVINE SONSHIP – John 1:12 *"Yet to all who received Him, to those who believed in His Name, He gave the right to become children of God."*

SPIRITUAL FULLNESS – Matthew 5:6 *"Blessed are those who hunger and thirst for righteousness for they will be filled."*

John 6:35 *"Then Jesus declared, 'I am the Bread of Life. He who comes to me will never go hungry, and he who believes in me will never be thirsty.'"*

SPIRITUAL POWER TO SERVE HIM – Acts 1:8 *"But you will receive power when the Holy Spirit comes on you: And you will be my witnesses in Jerusalem, and in all Judea and Samaria, and to the ends of the earth."*

John 14:12 *"I tell you the truth, anyone who has faith in me will do what I have been doing. He will do even greater things than these, because I am going to the Father."*

Peter is trying to help us to grasp a profound truth we need firmly engrained in our hearts and minds. His *"divine power has given us everything we need for life and godliness . . . He has given His very great and precious promises, so that through them you may participate in"* His nature now. We have been given provisions to see and understand, and to experience right now the glory and goodness of Jesus Christ in our daily lives that we may declare His praise and glory to this generation on this planet.

Our provisions for life and godliness are for today and they must be appropriated by faith now. Purity and godliness are foundational for serving the Lord right now in the town where you and I live today. He is looking for a Kingdom people who will be daily appropriating these very great and precious promises grasping them, claiming them, and in prayer inviting Him to fulfill them is us right now. His promises are precious to Him. He loves to hear them claimed in prayer inviting Him to divine intervention in us!

The Promises Bring a Divine Contrast

II Peter 1:4 *"Through these He has given us His very great and precious promises, so that through them you may participate in the divine nature and escape the corruption in the world caused by evil desires."*

Taken together and appropriated into the life of a person who has believed and received Jesus into his/her life, the power of His indwelling Holy Spirit, and the precious promises of God are the eternal salvation and transformation of we human beings and an absolutely awesome miracle takes shape and grows in us.

"YOU MAY PARTICIPATE IN THE DIVINE NATURE." We are given a new heart as a creation of God. He puts new desires in us and a new spirit in us who moves us to please our Eternal King.

We receive the new nature of our new family we bear the image of our Father God through Christ our King we take on a new family resemblance. We resemble the Lord our God as we surrender our hearts, our will, and our purposes in life for His will, character, and what He desires to do in and through us.

As a Hepner I got skinny legs, a big nose, and dark brown hair now turning whiter and whiter. The old adage is "the apple doesn't fall too far from the tree." Hepners are notorious teasers, who absolutely love to laugh, belly laugh, and I inherited that trait. I tried out for the part of Julius Teaser in my school play and won the part. My wife and I raised three teasers and now we have ten grandchildren who love to tease people. Pure coincidence I am sure.

I bear the marks of my earthly parentage, the family resemblance. As a child of God I got a new heart and a new mindset that compels me and constrains me in holy love to do my best to please God. I got new character traits that are being grown in me as fruit of His Spirit . . . *"love, joy, peace, gentleness, meekness, kindness, goodness, faithfulness and self-control"*

All of this has produced a divine contrast in my own life that is absolutely wonderful to me every time I think about it. As a child of my Father God in Christ, a royal subject in His Kingdom on planet earth here and now I have the great spiritual victory of also ESCAPING THE CORRUPTION of the world system caused by EVIL DESIRES:

Turning my back on this world system that wars against my new life in Christ . . . I *"have escaped"* (aorist tense a one time, completed action that's behind me) *the corruption in this world caused by evil desires."* That is my own fleshly wants that one time ruled me, so that I couldn't please God. That old nature I have "crucified with Christ".

And in contrast I am now given the incredibly wonderful privilege of sowing to His new heart, or the divine nature God miraculously created in me through Jesus Christ my King. There is a very real, present active union with Jesus in my life every day by His Holy Spirit who lives in me enabling, shaping, and empowering me to serve Him as a royal subject. This truth is one of the great pearls of God's revelation. I get to experience, right now in my daily life, the transforming power of knowing Jesus personally.

John 14:19b – 21 *"Because I live, you also will live. On that day you will realize that I am in my Father, and you are in me, and I am in you. Whoever has my commands and obeys them, he is the one who loves me. He who loves me will be loved by my Father, and I too will love him and show myself to him."*

Galatians 2:20 *"I have been crucified with Christ and I no longer live, but Christ lives in me. The life I live in the body, I live by faith in the Son of God who loved me and gave Himself for me."*

Romans 8:9 *"You, however, are not controlled by the sinful nature but by the Spirit, if the Spirit of God lives in you. And if anyone does not have the Spirit of Christ, he does not belong to Christ."*

What powerful truth we may embrace! Jesus has made it clear that He delights in His promises and is touched deeply when we stand on them, believe them, and pray them back to Him. This something in which God delights! God the Spirit desires that all of us embrace and stand on His promises to us as we seek to know Him more intimately than we presently do.

Here are my Hegai questions for you to ponder as we close this chapter on His precious promises. As you think about your life over the past twelve months, how important have the promises of God been to you? As you think about your life for the next twelve months, how important will these precious promises of God be to your spiritual journey now that we have worked on this truth together? Oh, how the King delights to hear His promises proclaimed from the lips of His sons and daughters who trust in Him.

Chapter Four

The Shed Blood of Jesus Christ

Let's simply state the fundamental thing we are thinking about as we walk along on our journey together. We're seeking to look at and answer the crucial kingdom question of devoted followers of Jesus Christ. What are the things that God the Father, Son, Holy Spirit, esteems as highly valued, very precious, of great worth in His sight?

As we look around us at our culture it becomes pretty obvious that there are some things that are highly esteemed, very precious, very valuable to people who have adopted this culture's philosophy. And, if we're completely honest these values are completely antithetical to the stated values of those who belong to the kingdom of God.

Culture's value is the ultimate inalienable right to have. We value consumerism, with its stated belief that, "You are what you have the ability to possess." Things like the right vocation and income, which produces social status, and the right house in the right section of town, German automobiles, and a Rolex instead of a Timex. All of these things that are valuable are things, material things.

Other values in our culture are things like individual rights and freedoms, amassing knowledge and expertise. The value states that to know more is to be a better person. I haven't found that value to be true in any sense of the word. Some of the most amoral people I have read have been highly educated and intelligent people! And let's not forget the latest self-help books and methodologies to help us have better self-esteem, better relationships, and tighter, less flabby bodies.

Not one of the above material things or self-help concepts is wrong or sinful in and of itself, but highly valuable and esteemed, precious and cherished? Hardly, among people who long to love and serve the Lord Jesus Christ. The truth is that the kingdom we have become part of is a radical call to live a holy life, a life that is set apart unto and under the Lordship of Jesus. To us consumerism is seen for what it really is: A life that is devoted to self-interest, which is the essence of sin.

As we walk together in this journey studying the things that are highly esteemed by God, we need to remember that we are people who profess to be Christians, who walk under the banner "Jesus is Lord." When Christ Jesus reached into our hearts and lives to save us, we were adopted into His family and now we are known by His characteristics and values, not ours. We become partakers of His Kingdom, the Kingdom of Heaven on earth, we became His royal subjects:

Jesus taught us about the value of being partakers of His kingdom in Matthew 14:44-46, and how His kingdom's value changes our perspective:

"The kingdom of heaven is like treasure hidden in a field. When a man found it, he hid it again, and then in his joy went and sold all he had and bought that field. And again the kingdom of heaven is like a merchant looking for fine pearls. When he found one of great value, he went away and sold everything he had and bought it."

When He gave those two precious stories, Jesus was driving at a point. To get all hung up about the propriety of buying a field without informing the owner of the treasure, is to totally miss the point Jesus wanted us to see and understand. The knowledge that we have come to enter the kingdom of heaven on earth is worth more than anything this world could ever offer to us as valuable. The King of this kingdom is my Lord and as Lord of my heart, He supersedes any other love, loyalty, or value.

That we have entered a relationship with the King of kings and Lord of lords by faith in Jesus Christ ought also then to move us to want to know more about this king. What does He love? What gives Him joy and delight? What is precious to Him? We'll want to find out how to practically love and please our king as His royal subjects.

It's a bit like a marriage Jesus said. He talked to us about the kingdom of Heaven being like a wedding feast for His Son that people are invited to. And He compared Himself to a bridegroom and His people to a bride. If you want to build a quality relationship of marriage with your spouse one of the things you will do is, in the normal process of give and take of married life you will learn what bugs your spouse and try to avoid those behaviors or habits. And on the other side of the same coin, you want to do what pleases them. Your love for them will move you to do those things.

God has clearly communicated to us that there are some things that are highly valued, very precious to Him. They are clearly communicated in His Word and if we truly love Him, if Jesus is really Lord, then we are going to grasp hold of those things and hold them as precious to our hearts too. Love for the Lord moves us to love what He loves, do what pleases Him, to hold as precious what He holds as precious.

In this chapter we are looking at another thing that God delights in, considers precious, highly esteems and values: The Shed Blood of Jesus Christ. Speaking by the Holy Spirit, Peter wrote, the following: I Peter 1:17 – 21 *"Since you call on a Father who judges each man's work impartially, live your lives as strangers here in reverent fear. For you know that it was not with perishable things such as silver or gold that you were redeemed from the empty way of life handed down to you from your forefathers, but with the precious blood of Christ, a lamb without blemish or defect. He was chosen before the creation of the world, but was revealed in these last times for your sakes. Through Him you believe in God who raised him from the dead and glorified Him and so your faith and hope are in God."*

Peter is talking about the very precious thing of our having been redeemed by the shed blood of Jesus Christ and he gives us two critical truths about what to and not to value:

1) Don't be friends or adopted into, lovers of this world's values – *"live your lives as strangers here in reverent fear"*

2) Focus not on what the world considers valuable, but on what God in Christ paid to redeem you from the curse of sin – *"it was not with perishable things such as silver or gold that you were redeemed"* . . . . *"but with the precious blood of Christ."*

It Took Perfect Blood to Redeem Us

Verse 19 ". . . .but with the precious blood of Christ, a Lamb without blemish or defect."

As one reads through the Old Testament one is struck by the sacrificial system that God instituted with His people Israel. The tabernacle and later the temple rites were set up around a very complex system of blood sacrifices offered on the altar by priests on behalf of people. The sacrifice offered to God, the blood of the animal that was shed gave to the worshipper a ceremonial cleansing from the sins he had committed.

The book of Hebrews teaches us that this sacrificial system was only a shadow of the good things to come to God's people through the once and for all sacrifice Jesus made for us.

Hebrews 10:2-4 *"the same sacrifices repeated endlessly year after year can never make perfect those who draw near to worship. If it could, would they not have stopped being offered? For the worshippers would have been cleansed once for all, and would no longer have felt guilty for their sins. But those sacrifices are an annual reminder of sins because it is impossible for the blood of bulls and goats to take away sins"*

However in that system, even though it is only a shadow of what was to come we were taught some tremendous principles:

Hebrews 9:22 *"The law requires that nearly everything be cleansed with blood, and without the shedding of blood there is not forgiveness."*

1) The redemption price for sin was the shedding of blood and not just any blood will do.

2) The blood had to be from a perfect, unblemished lamb, no defects.

3) The blood was shed by the innocent on behalf of the guilty.

Peter reminds us all of a biblical doctrine that is absolutely true. Our redemption was purchased for us at a very precious and expensive price: the *"precious blood of Christ, a Lamb without blemish or defect."* Jesus blood is precious because it is perfect, sinless, and innocent blood, the only thing that could redeem us from sin.

Scripture carefully protects that twin doctrines of the virgin birth of Christ Jesus to Mary both in prophecy before Christ's birth and in actuality in the New Testament. Likewise the doctrine that Jesus Christ was sinless and perfect so that He could be our sin offering, redeem us from the curse of sin, is protected by scripture in prophecy and actuality:

Hebrews 9:14 *"How much more then will the blood of Christ, who through the eternal Spirit offered Himself unblemished to God, cleanse our consciences from acts that lead to death, so that we may serve the living God."*

II Corinthians 5:21 *"God made Him who had no sin to be sin for us, so that in Him we might become the righteousness of God."*

In the Old Covenant a person would lay a little lamb on the altar and watch as its throat was slit and its blood drained away. It died in the stead of the worshipper to forgive the sins the worshipper had committed. The worshipper whose heart was tender had to be torn by the sight of a pure little innocent lamb giving its life because of his sin. It had to be a moving experience.

Christians are people who realize that outside Jerusalem Jesus Christ, Lamb of God took upon Himself, His innocent and pure life, the guilt, shame, and stain of our sins. Jesus chose to shed His blood and to die; the punishment of the death our sins deserve. Jesus took in our place. By faith we have been there and we have seen our sins, what we did to offend God laid on Christ Jesus, and we have seen Him become guilty of our transgressions. The Christian whose heart is tender can't help but be moved, torn in the heart at this pure and innocent Son of God dying for us! The blood of Christ is precious because it took perfect blood to redeem us!

It was Shed for Us in Love

Romans 5:6-8 *"You see, at just the right time, when we were still powerless, Christ died for the ungodly. Very rarely will anyone die for a righteous man, though for a good man someone might possibly dare to die. But God demonstrates His own love for us in this: While we were still sinners, Christ died for us."*

The second thing I'd like us to think about together, concerning the preciousness of the blood of Christ in the eyes of God, is that it was shed in an act of sacrificial love and self-emptying love. Paul clearly brings out in this scripture from Romans 5 that Christ Jesus died for us. He shed His blood on the cross in holy, giving love.

Scripture carefully protects the truth that it was love that brought Jesus into the earth. It was love that caused Him to become a man and it was love that caused Him to enter the plight, the dilemma of human sin. He knew we were sinners and hopelessly headed for eternal hell with no way to be saved from it. So in love He chose to come and die on our behalf.

Scripture also carefully teaches us, a very important truth about the shedding of His blood. Jesus was not murdered by the Jews or the Roman authorities. No one on planet earth had enough power or might to crucify the Lord of glory had He chosen not to go to the cross.

He told Peter in the garden – *"Put your sword back in its place, for all who draw the sword will die by the sword. Do you think I cannot call on my Father and he will at once put at my disposal more than twelve legions of angels? But how then would the scriptures be fulfilled that say it must happen this way?"*

In teaching the Jewish leaders about true discipleship to God and true love for God He told them, John 10:17,18 – *"The reason my Father loves me is that I lay down my life-only to take it up again. No one takes it from me, but I lay it down of my own accord. I have authority to lay it down and authority to take it up again. This command I received from my Father."*

When Jesus' blood was shed on the cross it was done in the most magnificent act of love for others the world has ever or will ever see. We see love moving the heart of Jesus in the Garden. He didn't want to become guilty of our sin and shame but moved Him to pray – *"Not my will but your will be done, Father."* Love put Jesus on the cross for us; it wasn't soldiers or the Sanhedrin.

In His death on the cross holy, giving love stoops to bear all of our sins and die our death – love taking our place so that we might go free from sin and death by faith in Him! Jesus' blood is precious because it was shed in love for you and me, and when it touches us by faith, the prayer He prayed for forgiveness, while shedding His blood for us becomes a reality! His love brings forgiveness.

It Washes Us of Sin and Shame

I Peter 1:18, 19 (selected) *"You were redeemed from the empty way of life handed down to you from your forefathers, by the precious blood of Christ . . . ."*

Revelation 1:5b, 6 *"To Him who loves us and has freed us from our sins by His blood, and has made us to be a kingdom and priests to serve His God and Father – to Him be glory and power for ever and ever! Amen."*

I Peter 2:24, 25 *"He Himself bore our sins in His body on the tree, so that we might die to sins and live to righteousness; by His wounds you have been healed. For you were like sheep going astray, but now you have returned to the Shepherd and Over-seer of your souls."*

It is an incredible thing to think through, tremendously moving, but it is doctrinally true according to the scriptures. There is only one thing that can wash away the sins of people, take them away, forgive them, and completely cleanse the heart and mind of all the shame, stain, and guilt of sin. That one thing is the precious blood of Christ.

The reason the blood of Christ has power to forgive, wash, and cleanse is that He was a perfect, sinless sacrifice and He chose to permit God our Father to lay upon Him all of the sinfulness and wickedness of all people. Jesus the perfect Son of God died, shed His blood, while being loaded down with my sins and yours on the cross. There on the cross He is our sin bearer, our sacrificial Lamb. He completes God's holy requirement for a perfect sacrifice for me, once and for all. He completes God's holy requirement for the shedding of blood for the forgiveness cleansing of sins.

Consequently today, 2000 years later, Jesus can say to you and me: "Son, daughter I bore your sins for you on the cross. I shed my blood for you on the cross. I died in your stead on the cross and if you will believe in me and will receive me as Savior and Lord I will cleanse you of all sin's stain, and of its ability to control you!

The blood of Christ Jesus is precious because it alone washes people of sin's stain.

It Destroys the Enemy's Power to Control Us

Revelation 12:10,11a *"Now have come the salvation and the power and the kingdom of our God, and the authority of His Christ. For the accuser of our brothers, who accuses them before our God day and night, has been hurdled down. They overcame him by the blood of the Lamb and the word of their testimony.*

The fourth thing I want us to see together about the blood of Christ that deems it precious in God's sight is that it destroys Satan's power to control our lives any more. What are the enemy's tools to use on people to hold them into his power and bondage? They are sin and death. By shedding His blood for us Jesus cleanses all of us who believe in Him, of sin-our guilt and stain is removed!

Furthermore, by dying for us in our place, He died to sins once for all so that all who believe in Him shall not die eternal death, but have eternal life in Christ. Because God our Father raised Him from the dead and seated Him at His right hand on the throne we know this sacrifice is acceptable for the removal of sin and death's bondage. Jesus promised us, "Because I live you too shall live." In Christ Jesus' life we have eternal life now and forever. Satan has no right, no place to stand in the life of a blood-bought and blood-washed child of God. His two big tools, sin and death, have been destroyed in the Christian's life by faith in Jesus Christ!

You and I have been made more than conquerors through the precious blood of Jesus. We have overcome the enemy's ability to rule us or enslave us by the blood of the Lamb and the word of our testimony! "I am His and He is mine!"

When, not if, we are tempted to sin or to turn away from the Lord God, we do not have to stand in our own strength and attempt to win against temptation. God has provided for us a better way. When we are assaulted by feelings of condemnation for things the Lord has already cleansed us of, for which we are forgiven, we don't have to fight it on our own strength. God has provided for us a better way. When we are accused, oppressed by the dark night of the soul, and beaten down by the onslaught of the enemy's work against us, it is important to remember that we don't have to stand against the enemy in our own power.

God has provided a better way for us to stand in victory. It is the precious blood of Jesus Christ His Son our Savior that has washed us and cleansed us, and purified us of all unrighteousness. We overcome all of the malignant works of the enemy by the blood of the Lamb and by the word of our testimony! You are not alone! You are not out on a limb! You have a Victor living in your heart by faith! Consequently, you have victory over the darkness! Recently I have been teaching the church family I pastor to make a confession in times when they sense the enemy is working to get them to turn away from the provisions of God. The confession goes like this:

> "I am the son/daughter of the Most High God. My Abba Father has adopted me as His child. I have been bought with the precious blood of Jesus. The Spirit of the living God lives in my heart. I take my primary identity from who I am in Christ and not from my human ancestry."

Well, my dear fellow traveler on this journey of faith we call the Christian life, you are now in possession of another truth, another thing that is precious to God and therefore must become precious to you and me. He wants us to treat the blood of His Son Jesus as a precious commodity to be cherished in our hearts. That means He wants us to make sure we don't treat the blood Jesus shed to redeem us as something to be trivialized, or that we turn our backs on what He has done and flirt with sin. In Hebrews 10:26 – 29, the Hebrew author tells us that when we choose to deliberately sin we treat the blood that saved us as common, unholy, and profane. When we do so we insult the Spirit of God. May we never again make such choices to turn our backs on the blood that saved us! May you and I cherish what He has done for us for the rest of our lives!

My Hegai heart longs to have you ask and answer a simple question: How important is the precious blood of Jesus to you, in your daily life? There are some companion questions on my mind as well. When you are tempted to sin, or worse to deliberately choose sin, is the blood Jesus shed for you one of the first things you think about? Now that we have looked at these truths together in this chapter, how important will the blood of Jesus be to you for the next twelve months?

Chapter Five

His Redeemed People

Believers in Christ Jesus are people who have been redeemed by the precious blood of Jesus, and have become partakers of His kingdom on earth right now. It is really important to ask and answer very well this question we have been studying together: What are the things that are precious to God Almighty our Lord and King?

The reason for asking that question is very simple. We are called to walk through life in an intimate relationship with the Lord. How do we increase relational love with another person? We learn to know them better, the things they love, what makes them tick, what they consider to be precious and highly valued. If you really want to learn to know a person you ask them quality questions and listen carefully to what they share of themselves with you. Knowing these things about them increases our understanding of them and widens the basis of our relationship with them.

The Lord has made it very clear to us in His Word what is precious to Him. We can take this knowledge of God's heart, delights, what God values and esteems and we can choose to hold as precious to us what delights God. If we know what makes our King's heart smile and what causes Him joy, we can know some things we can give ourselves to in order to increase our relationship with Him as Lord and Master.

It's also extremely important to embrace the basic understanding that the world system or cultural values we find ourselves living in are very often the absolute opposite of God's kingdom values! We've noted that our cultural values, that is what is esteemed in the world system, is often the outward, the material, and the fleshly.

It is also true the conditioning of our ears, how we hear and decide, or put another way the set of filters through which we perceive things is founded on our North American value of independence. We value being able to decide for ourselves what is right and what is wrong. We don't like being told what to do, where to go, and what to think. In our culture self-determination, "I decide what is right for me," is the key value. The language of Scripture is Kingdom language in which God in Christ Jesus is King and we are His servants. Our hearts must be changed from our cultural values, our rugged individualism and our independence if we are going to be able to hear His words of instruction and His commands as loving subjects.

We've noted that cultural values are the outward and material. People in North America are assigned status and esteem on things that do not have much to do with what really matters. Culture values things like the right house in the right neighborhood, the right car – German instead of American made – and the outward signs of success. These values have little to do with anything that really matters, like caring for those who can't care for themselves, like loving people and walking through life with integrity of heart whether or not people can see our behaviors.

We've noted that as those who have been saved, we have become a part of His royal Kingdom right here and now on planet earth. As members of His Kingdom, royal subjects we have been given throne room privileges of prayer in Jesus Christ our Lord and it is very wise for us to spend time with our King in His throne room so that we'll have His individual marching orders for our lives.

In this chapter we are looking at a fourth thing that is precious to God: **His Redeemed Children**, His church as a bride preparing herself now for her day of wedding consummation. The truth is that all of us who are believers in Christ Jesus are God's adopted sons and daughters; you and I are precious to God.

Isaiah 43:1-5 *"But now, this is what the Lord says – he who created you, O Jacob, He who formed you, O Israel; 'Fear not for I have redeemed you: I have summoned you by name; you are mine. When you pass through the waters, I will be with you; and when you pass through the rivers, they will not sweep over you. When you walk through the fire you will not be burned; the flames will not set you ablaze. For I am the Lord, your God, the Holy One of Israel; your Savior; . . . Since you are precious and honored in my sight, and because I love you, I will give men in exchange for you, and people in exchange for your life. Do not be afraid for I am with you;"*

Malachi 3:17, 18 *"They will be mine, says the Lord Almighty, in the day when I make up my treasured possession. I will spare them, just as in compassion a man spares his son who serves him. And you will again see the distinction between the righteous and the wicked, between those who serve God and those who do not."*

Ephesians 5:1, 2 *"Be imitators of God, therefore as dearly loved children and live a life of love, just as Christ loved us and gave Himself up for us as a fragrant offering and sacrifice to God."*

In each of those 3 Scriptures it comes through loudly and clearly that God's people, those who are His redeemed sons and daughters, that would be you and me, are very precious, of inestimable value in the sight of God.

In Malachi 3 the Lord is talking things over with His man Malachi and He describes a group of people who will know Him and who will walk through life choosing to reverently fear Him, honor and esteem Him. In Malachi 3:17 there is a word about how God feels toward those people whom He has spared and upon whom He has showered compassion. I don't think it is a stretch to the text at all to place these words as prophetic words for you and me, as the redeemed of the Lord, to see ourselves as His "treasured possession." We are loved, treasured, and precious to God's heart because of our eternal redemption in Christ Jesus.

In Ephesians 4 Paul is writing to the church at Ephesus about the people who have come to know Jesus personally and deeply, the sons and daughters of God in Christ Jesus. He teaches on our unity in Christ, that we are called to work together in love, and that we are called to embrace and exhibit His new nature and attitudes are alive in us. In Ephesians 5:1 when Paul writes to the people of God he refers to us as, *"as dearly loved children."* The words he chose to express how God our Father feels about us is the Greek the words are tekna agapeta – children of the age of accountability, old enough to know right from wrong, who are loved with holy, deep, self-giving love by God.

As we continue this study and seek to embrace what we see in God's heart of love for His redeemed, the Lord has laid on my heart four things that help us to unpack the understanding that we, His people, are precious to Him.

The Price of Our Redemption

Ephesians 5:1, 2 *"Be imitators of God, therefore, as dearly loved children and live a life of love, just as Christ loved us and gave Himself up for us as a fragrant offering and sacrifice to God."*

Isaiah 43:1 *"Fear not for I have redeemed you; I have summoned you by name, you are mine"*.

Malachi 3:17 *"They will be mine' says the Lord Almighty, 'in the day when I make them my treasured possession. I will spare them' . . ."*

God has spoken about our eternal salvation in Christ Jesus in promise in Isaiah 43:1 and Malachi 3:17 when he says through his prophet Isaiah *"I have redeemed you, you are mine,"* and through Malachi calls us God's treasured possession whom He will spare. We receive one of the greatest words of promise and love we could ever hear. God says to all of us who are adopted sons and daughters that we will all receive loving mercy and protection. We will be spared.

But notice with me in the text from Ephesians 5:1, 2 that there is One in the universe who is God's Son, Jesus the Incarnate Word, the Son made flesh and dwelling among us. He is God's One and Only Son not by adoption, but by nature and in likeness. He is God's One and Only Son, in a relation to God the Father which no other could occupy. There is none other like the brilliance of this Jesus, no other Incarnate Son of God, who served His Father completely in perfect love and obedience.

As parents we feel incredible love for our children, we want the best for them, we care deeply about their welfare, and we give expecting nothing in return because our parental love runs very deep. But who of us can measure or begin to understand the love of God the Father for His One and Only Son Jesus Christ.

Surely, because God wants all of His children "to be happy in Jesus," as the Son of God comes to earth, the Father will insure His blessings in life, He will see to His Son's protection and joy all the days of His earthly life. Surely God the Father will anoint Him with oil of gladness, and permit no sorrow to touch His brow. Surely no clouds of difficulty will overshadow the Son of God!

But that is not the way things transpired is it? Scripture teaches us that our Father's love was so great for we who were sinners that He *"spared not His own Son, but delivered Him up for us all."* His deep love and mercy for us sinful people made Him willing to sacrifice His One and Only Son Jesus. When we read the words of John 3:16 *"For God so loved the world that He gave His One and Only Son"* . . . or the words of Romans 5:8 *"But God demonstrates His own love for us in this: While we were still sinners Christ died for us"* . . . our hearts should be, need to be deeply moved at the price of our redemption.

God the Father fully knew the travail Jesus would experience when He said these words of promise to Malachi: *"I will make them my treasured possession . . . I will spare them."* He knew the horror Jesus would experience at having all of our sins laid upon Him as He died on the cross yet *"He spared not His Own Son"* so He could spare us and make us His redeemed treasured possession.

As we think about our being precious, dearly loved by God our Father, we must remember the price of our redemption Jesus paid for us in the will of His Father. How deeply moving to know we are loved by God that much!

Knowing We Are Precious to God Gives Us A Place of Strength to Stand

As you walk into bookstores you see a tremendous amount of self-help books or books that give counsel on how to build one's self-esteem, how to feel better about yourself. It's pretty apparent, or at least it should be, that the cultural value of expressing yourself and embracing the message of self-interest has left us with several generations of people that are struggling to achieve a healthy self-concept.

We are told by secular pop-psychology that we need to experience positive self-esteem. There are hosts of people teaching what is assumed to be truth but it really isn't when one analyzes it carefully in light of Scripture. The teaching goes that "Jesus died to give us positive self-esteem." The truth is that Jesus died to give us God's esteem as adopted sons and daughter, and given the choice between positive self-esteem and knowing God's esteem I will always choose the latter. The truth is that we really aren't capable of pulling ourselves up by our bootstraps and delivering the message that we're OK, we're good stuff.

That being said, the child of God has come to learn of a deeper healing than self-help band-aide therapy. The child of God has come by faith to the cross of Jesus, admitted his or her sin and utter helplessness with a broken and contrite heart, and the child of God has thrown him/herself on the Mercy Seat of God. And from the Throne of Grace, from the Spirit of God Almighty, the child of God has heard these words:

"Fear not for I have redeemed you; I have called you by Name, you are mine. I am the Lord your God the Holy One, your Savior, . . . Since you are precious to me and because I love you I give" (my Son Jesus as a ransom for you)

"On that day I make you my treasured possession. I spare your life".

"Be imitators of God therefore as dearly loved children, and live a life of love just as Christ loved us and gave Himself up for us as a fragrant offering and sacrifice to God".

Talk about inner health and a view of the self – a self-concept that is positive. People who are God's children in Christ need only to perceive and receive God's viewpoint of us to be healed and whole, healthy in the heart.

I take you back again to the analogy that living in God's Kingdom is often compared analogously to a healthy marriage. Think with me about a positive and healthy marriage relationship between two people who truly love each other. No matter what may come, what storms of life may descend upon them, their home is a safe haven amidst storms of life. Because there is a woman named Raina in my life, there is a person who loves me and into whose arms I can retreat. I have a safe and secure place to stand. My spouse thinks I'm precious. To her there's no one quite like me. I can entrust myself to her.

For every child of God the Biblical picture is that Jesus is our groom and we're His bride. In His sight we are precious, treasured, dearly loved. Amidst the hard places of life, when there are storms and the heart hurts there is a Comforter into whose love we can retreat. Because we're precious to God we have a safe place to stand! In God's arms there is security and strength!

As God's Beloved Precious Possession, We Are Gifted

Again I take you to the analogy of the Kingdom of God being compared to a good quality relationship between a husband and a wife to share another truth with you relative to our being precious, dearly loved by God our Father in Christ Jesus our Lord. When a person really is head-over-heels in love with his/her spouse they absolutely delight to give that person gifts, to do little things for them that will enrich and develop their lives, and that will bring a smile of love and appreciation to their face and joy to their hearts.

If he enjoys red velvet cake, or vanilla whoopie pies, or chocolate marble cake with cherry icing she makes these for him periodically and surprises him with them when he comes home. And when he's hurting she gives him the precious gift of loving, kind words to make him feel her love and genuine support.

If she enjoys a surprise Chinese take-out lunch, or holding hands in front of an old movie Friday night, or the surprise of the dishes being done with no pleading, he will give these gifts to her because of his love for her. When she hurts he will give her the hugs and do the holding she needs expecting nothing in return.

Because you and I are precious to God He has given each of us special gifts too, as His treasured, dearly loved children. Some of His natural gifts and abilities it seems we can easily take for granted. Things like intelligence, health, family, or the natural aptitudes and abilities or talents we each have to work with our hands, paint a picture, or play a sport, or understand science readily.

God also has given each of us supernatural gifts of the Holy Spirit who lives in our hearts and lives. Each one of us has at least one supernatural gift of the Holy Spirit which when used in the context of all of the other people of the local body of Christ causes the church to be built up, strengthened, and unified in Christ. God gives people supernatural mercy, helps, teaching, serving, giving, counseling, shepherding, and leading. He has given some supernatural communication gifts -- encouraging, exhorting, prophesying, words of wisdom, words of knowledge, preaching, teaching, tongues and interpreting tongues.

Romans12:4 - 6a *"Just as each of us has many members, and these members do not all have the same function, so in Christ we who are many form one body, and each member belongs to all the others. We have different gifts, according to the grace given to us"*. . .

Ephesians 4:16 *"From him (Jesus Christ) the whole body, joined and held together by every supporting ligament, grows and builds itself up in love as each part does its work."*

Because we are precious, treasured possessions, dearly loved by God, we are given natural and supernatural gifts and when we use those gifts for His glory He blesses us tremendously and the whole church is built up!

Because We're Precious to God We Can Learn to Love One Another Deeply

I Peter 1:22 *"Now that you have purified yourselves by obeying the truth so that you have sincere love for your brothers, love one another deeply, from the heart."*

We need to go back to this issue of our being fellow royal subjects in the Kingdom of God on earth and each one of us, as His possession, is dearly loved by Him. If we are truly treasured by God, then we can learn to treasure, respect, and appreciate one another, as fellow subjects, in His kingdom on earth!

It is so fitting for Peter to write about loving other people deeply from the heart because Peter was a man who constantly erected barriers between himself and others he would not or could not love; Peter's barriers were often racial or religious prejudice.

In Acts 10:9-15 Peter received a very convicting vision about eating food that was considered unlawful to Jews, and was therefore considered to be unclean. God told him to eat some ham and reptile meat . . . Verses 14, 15 *"Surely not Lord!' Peter replied. "I have never eaten anything impure or unclean.' The voice spoke to him a second time, 'Do not call anything impure that God has made clean.'"*

The next day Peter understood clearly that the vision wasn't about food at all, it was about our view of other people whom the Holy Spirit is dealing with in change in their lives. Acts 10:34, 35 *"I now realize how true it is that God does not show favoritism but accepts men from every nation who fear Him and do what is right"*. . . .

Peter was taught an incredibly important lesson and we need to learn it as well. Barriers that we have responsibilities for erecting between ourselves and other people on the basis of skin color, race, background, theological persuasion, education, or their personality are wrong. These things tend to label and demean another person for whom Christ Jesus died. We must make the choice of the heart to systematically, in genuine repentance, dismantle these attitudes and destroy them in our hearts. To do this will require that you and I invest time with in building relationships with people we wouldn't normally invest time in. This is a kingdom ethic to be embraced, brothers and sisters.

You know it is so easy to erect relational barriers to others, choosing not to love, by focusing on what is wrong, what we don't like, or on our conceptions or perceptions. It is hard work to decide to love others so deeply that every time we sense we're building a barrier to loving to take it down from our side of the wall.

Defensiveness, apprehension, disagreement all build walls and barriers to genuine loving are the easy, natural relational road traveled far too often by God's people. The truth is that, as a general rule the easy, natural road is not God's road.

Loving despite differences, looking for truth and looking for commonalities to build on, endeavoring to keep the unity of the Spirit in the bond of peace, that's hard to do but it's also God's Kingdom supernatural road.

Peter learned at Cornelius' house that what God loves, redeemed people whom the Holy Spirit of God is at work in, are to be loved and treated with the same grace that we have received in Christ Jesus. God considers all kinds of people from all cultures, race, and personality type, to be precious in His sight, His treasured possession.

So here comes my Hegai counsel to you before we conclude this chapter: Are you making the effort to treat everyone with the basics of love and respect? I know some folks are harder to love than others. But if they are precious to God then they must be precious to God's people. This is especially true of all of your brothers and sisters in Christ. If **all** of the redeemed people of God in Christ Jesus are precious to God then they must **all** be precious to us too. We must constantly make the choice to do what we can to take down any and every barrier we have erected. That's an individual choice we each must make in our hearts.

Because we are precious to God we can and must learn to *"love one another deeply from the heart."*

Chapter Six

Obedience to His Commands

In the last chapter we looked at the fact that God's people are His treasured possession, of great value, highly esteemed in His sight. It is another answer to our key kingdom question we are asking in this study: What are the things that are valued, highly esteemed and precious to God?

The reason for asking that question is very simple. If we know from His Word what is precious to God and we are His royal subjects we will know what must also become highly valued to us.

I simply want to remind you that we are talking about things we are invited to know, understand, and embrace in our hearts as the followers of Jesus today. We are each involved in a battle for the allegiance of and the contents of what we cherish in our hearts. We are each responsible to be the gatekeepers of our own hearts, that is we choose what desires we embrace and what desires we reject. Remember Solomon's words of warning in Proverbs 4:23 *"Above all else guard your heart for it is the wellspring of life."*

We've noted that our cultural setting and values are based on expressing one's individual rights and privileges, of making important life chooses on the basis of "what's in it for me." The truth is that we are North Americans and we don't like to be told what to do, where we may or may not go, and we'll decide for ourselves what is best for our life. The language of Scripture is Kingdom language in which God in Christ Jesus is King and we are His servants. We take this posture gladly because we have given to Him our love. Our ears and hearts must hear His words of instruction and command as loving subjects and to do that well requires that we choose to repent of our cultural conditioning that leans us toward self-sufficiency and self-reliance.

We've noted that as members of His Kingdom, we have been given throne room privileges of prayer in Jesus Christ our Lord and it is very wise for us to spend time with our King in His throne room so that we'll have His individual marching orders for our lives. Alone with God, in prayer, fasting in prayer, and in the Scriptures, we'll be led to make choices inspired by loving gratitude to this King Jesus. Love moves us to want to please Him in lifestyle!

So far we have studied four things that our King considers to be very precious, highly esteems: Brokenness and contrition of heart, the precious blood of Jesus Our Lord, His promises found in the Scriptures and His redeemed people.

As we look to the Word of God for another thing that our Lord God and King Eternal considers precious, treasures, dearly loves – we are looking at **Obedience** in the lives of His royal subjects.

The truth is that we have come to know Jesus as Lord and Savior. We have been made to be members of His Kingdom on earth now. As His royal subjects we have access into His eternal throne room through our trust in what Jesus has done for us. We need to see and understand that a King delights in servants who do what he says. God delights in obedience in His people. God's heart is filled with joy when His children demonstrate love and loyalty by doing what He asks, not because of any selfishness in His heart, because He doesn't have any, but because His will is for our best.

Exodus 19:5 *"Now if you obey me fully and keep my covenant, then out of all nations you will be my treasured possession. Although the whole earth is mine."*

John 14:23 *"Jesus replied, 'If anyone loves me, he will obey my teaching. My Father will love him, and we will come to him and make our home with him.'"*

What do we mean when we say God delights in a life of obedience in His people? Is it that God has placed a legal set of rules, a list of dos and don'ts and says if you do these things you are precious and if you don't do them you are cursed? No. To say that God delights in, finds precious a life of obedience in His children is to simply communicate that God is looking for a surrendered, submitted heart attitude in His people. God treasures His time with a son or daughter who will give the Holy Spirit free reign to teach, rebuke, train, and command and will apply God's Word to his/her life daily.

Obedience is not a condition of our salvation, as if to say, "if I do these things I'm truly saved and if I don't I'm not. Our works do not save us, we are saved by grace in Christ and then we can obey. And being obedient doesn't change our being loved by God. We are loved with an everlasting love from the womb of our mother. God's love for us is one absolute constant in our lives regardless of what we have done or not done.

No. God delights in obedience and makes His home in His people who obey because our obedience, permitting Him to have His way in our daily lives, is a living demonstration to God, ourselves, and the world that is watching us that we love Him as King. God says that obedience is a sacrifice that smells sweet to Him; it's a sacrifice of a loving heart. Yet thousands of sincere believers find themselves going days without a meaningful devotional time of prayer and Scripture study not by decision or a willful disobedience -- but by slippage, erosion of disciplines by default.

There's an interesting story about sacrifice and obedience from King Saul's life that illustrates this slippage or slow erosion in the king's life. God had clearly communicated His will to Saul through Samuel the prophet concerning the Amalekites; they were so wicked they were to be utterly destroyed. But Saul didn't do what he was told, he brought back plunder . . .

I Samuel 15:22 *"Does the Lord delight in burnt offerings and sacrifices as much as in obeying the Lord? To obey is better than sacrifice and to heed is better than the fat of rams."*

Saul's obedience eroded and he tried to make up for it with sacrifices to God. That never works. Often we can fall into the same erosion or slippage trap if we're not careful we can be tempted to use sacrifices we do for God in place of an obedient heart. We reason that we'll serve on one more committee at church, go to one more meeting, do one more good deed as a substitute for sitting down with our Bible, our notebook, taking time to talk things over with the Lord in prayer, and listening to what the Lord says to us that we might obey His holy marching orders for our life!

God our Father and Eternal King delights in our choice to surrender to Him, to give Him the gift of a submissive spirit or attitude because we love Him as His special sons and daughters. When we take time daily to engage with the Word of God it is a demonstration to Him that we see ourselves as His treasured possession!

Obedience Modeled in Jesus

John 15:10 *"If you obey my commands you will remain in my love, just as I have obeyed my Father's commands and remain in His love."*

The Gospel of John is a book about Jesus being the Son of God and woven throughout the text of the Gospel is a thread that demands that we all take a very serious look at it. Jesus Christ, the Son of God came to this earth to do the will of His heavenly Father. He came here to obey, fill up and complete the will of our Father God!

John 4:34 *"My food . . . is to do the will of Him who sent me and to finish His work."*

John 5:19 *"I tell you the truth, the Son can do nothing by Himself; He can only do what He sees His father doing, because whatever the Father does the Son also does."*

John 6:37, 38 *"All that the Father gives me will come to me, and whoever comes to me I will never drive away. For I have come down from heaven not to do my will but the will of Him who sent me."*

John 14:31 *"The world must learn that I love the Father and that I do exactly what my Father has commanded me."*

Over and over John rings out verses that teach us the same truth: Jesus Christ demonstrated for us just how precious it is in the sight of God our Father to be an obedient son or daughter. The way He chose to live His life in complete obedience to the Father, including His incredible suffering, shedding His own blood for our salvation, is a picture of how precious is obedience to the Father God's revealed will.

Jesus tells us here in this verse, in John 15:10, that when we choose to live a life of obedience it is very precious to Him and our Father God, in the very same way that He modeled for us. His life of obedience to God's complete will for His life was precious to the Father, *"just as I have obeyed My Father's commands and remain in His love."*

For me it is the Hebrew author who really fleshes this truth out and carries it to it's logical, spiritual conclusion, when in discussing the obedience of Jesus to the Father's will for His life He writes: Hebrews 5:7, 8 *"During the days of Jesus' life on earth, He offered up prayers and petitions with loud cries and tears to the one who could save Him from death, and He was heard because of His reverent submission. Although He was a son He learned obedience from what He suffered."*

For our Lord Jesus Christ surrender to the Father's will, loving obedience was extremely costly. It cost Him His perfect sinless blood that He shed on the cross for us. The Father's will sometimes carries an incredibly high price tag. Obedience wasn't easy for Jesus. He learned obedience from what He suffered. If that was true for God's One and Only Son by nature, as He lived here on earth, it will be true for sons and daughters of God today. We too will learn the depth of obedience when, at times, it is hard to do so.

Obedience Demonstrates that God's Heart Lives in Our Heart

John 15:10 *"If you obey my commands you will remain in my love, just as I have obeyed my Father's commands and remain in His love."* And verse 14 *"You are my friends if you do what I command."*

John 14:21 *"Whoever has my commands and obeys them, he is the one who loves me. He who loves me will be loved by my Father, and I too will love him and show myself to him."*

There is a very important sequence of events here that we must be careful not to miss or we will very much misunderstand what is being taught here. We must remember that obedience to God is a demonstration that our hearts have been changed. Obedience to God is not our natural inclination of our human nature. Making the choice every day to cooperate with His Holy Spirit, as His agenda made clear to us is a demonstration that God has changed our hearts.

Scripture carefully protects the doctrine, that a new heart living in us is a creation of God Almighty when we come to Him by faith and experience the gift of His salvation. We bow at the foot of the cross, repent of our sins, and ask Jesus to forgive us, cleanse us, and come into our lives, and He creates a new heart in us.

God does not reform our sinful nature or our self-centered tendencies of the heart. He doesn't reform what He says must be crucified and put to death in Christ Jesus. Nor does He simply cover our hearts of stone with a cleansing act of Jesus' blood. God makes our hearts brand new, creates in us a clean heart!

Ezekiel 36:26, 27 *"I will give you a new heart and put a new spirit in you; I will remove from you your heart of stone and give you a heart of flesh. I will put my spirit in you and move you to follow my decrees and be careful to keep my laws."*

II Corinthians 5:17 *"Therefore, if anyone is in Christ, he is a new creation; the old has gone, the new has come."*

The Lord is saying a powerful thing to the seeking heart? His royal subjects are not merely reformed, nor are their old hearts washed by the blood of Jesus and restored. All of us who know Jesus Christ as Savior and Lord have been given a new heart and that heart deeply desires to obey its King – Jesus Christ. As Paul was writing to the Roman believers about this incredible life-change the Holy Spirit does, in Romans 12:1, 2 he used a word to describe it that is awesome: metamorphousthe. It is the Greek word from which we get our word metamorphosis, "to radically alter the state of being, to transform the structure of one thing to another, a striking change in form or character." Once a caterpillar transforms into a butterfly it never reverts again, it is finished with its slimy existence!

Consequently we need to see that an obedient heart, cooperating with God's Holy Spirit who radically changes us from within is a demonstration that we are in fact truly saved, royal subjects of our King – Jesus Christ. We bear the marks of His new nature living in us, a nature that longs to obey and honor God the Father. There are at least 3 ways obedience is a demonstration:

a. <u>First</u> – Obedience demonstrates that the love of God lives in us.

b. <u>Second</u> – Obedience demonstrates the right heart of submission to God lives in us!

c. <u>Third</u> – Obedience demonstrates that we really are God's sons and daughters to our world that needs to know Him . . .

John 15:7, 8 *"If you remain in me and my words remain in you, ask whatever you wish, and it will given you. This is to my Father's glory, that you bear much fruit, showing yourselves to be my disciples."*

Obedience, cooperating with God's Holy Spirit as He opens up the Word to us is precious to God, because it demonstrates the heart of God is now living in us.

Obedience Gives Us Throne Room Privileges

John 15:7 *"If you remain in me and my words remain in you, ask whatever you wish, and it will be given you."*

John 15:16, 17 *"You did not choose me but I chose you and appointed you to go and bear fruit, fruit that will last. Then the Father will give you whatever you ask in my name. This is my command: love each other."*

The third thing we need to see about obedience being precious to God takes us back to our King and his court, our throne room analogy of kingdom living. In the natural realm when a king has a special servant who loves him deeply and does the king's bidding, who knows the king's heart and seeks to please the king sometimes without needing to be told there is a very special love between them that is evident in the court room.

That special servant has moved to a deep kindred heart of love for his king and, in many ways, is more like a friend to the king than a servant. In the Scriptures we are given special glimpses into this kind of relationship between a king and a very special servant in the lives of Joseph and Pharaoh, Nehemiah and Artaxerxes, and Daniel and Nebuchadnezzar. The king's scepter is always out to his dear servant friend. The servant friend can ask just about anything of his king and receive it because of his love for the king demonstrated by his lifestyle.

That is a meager, human analogy or way of saying in word picture what our Master and King Jesus communicates to us, His royal subjects, about our lives of obedience giving us throne room privileges in the throne room of our God in heaven. When we demonstrate, by lifestyle, obedience to our Father God in Christ and love to serve Him, delight ourselves in walking in His ways we are servant friends. We are special to God and when we walk into His presence, day or night, the scepter of open and loving communication is always extended to us!

Jesus told His trusted followers on the night of His betrayal some powerful words about friendship with Him. John communicates this powerful truth to us in John 15:7 – 16. Notice in this passage of Scripture that obedience and throne room privileges with God are linked not once but twice.

"If you remain in me and my words remain in you, ask whatever you wish, and it will be given you. This is to my Father's glory, that you bear much fruit, showing yourselves to be my disciples. As the Father has loved me, so have I loved you. Now remain in my love. If you obey my commands, you will remain in my love, just as I have obeyed my Father's commands and remain in his love. I have told you this so that my joy may be in you and that your joy may be complete. My command is this: Love each other as I have loved you. Greater love has no one than this, that he lay down his life for his friends. You are my friends if you do what I command. I no longer call you servants, because a servant does not know his master's business. Instead, I have called you friends, for everything that I learned from my Father I have made known to you. You did not choose me, but I chose you and appointed

you to go and bear fruit – fruit that will last. Then the Father will give you whatever you ask in my name. This is my command: Love each other."

God the Holy Spirit whispers His will and purposes to His friends, who choose to make the time to be alone with Him in the throne room and touch the scepter of His acceptance. He makes a passage of Scripture spring to life, or whispers by His still small voice, or speaks through a song, or a friend. My personal favorite listener's Psalm is Psalm 25.

Psalm 25:8, 9 *"Good and upright is the Lord; therefore he instructs sinners in his ways. He guides the humble in what is right and teaches them his way."*

Psalm 25:12 *"Who then is the man that fears the Lord? He will instruct him in the way chosen for him."*

Psalm 25:14, 15 *"The Lord confides in those who fear him; he makes his covenant known to them. My eyes are ever on the Lord, for only he will release my feet from the snare."*

So my Hegai counsel to you as we close this chapter is this. Have you thought about how important living a life of loving obedience really is as you consider your life in the courtroom of your king? Living lifestyles of loving obedience to the revealed will of God means that we have been given heavenly throne room privileges right now. We can ask for anything in the context of His will and receive it. Obedience, cooperating with God's Holy Spirit as He opens up the Word to us, is so precious to God He grants us throne room privileges. When He sees us in the outer court His face lights up and He holds out to us the royal scepter. "Good morning Ken. I have been waiting for you. What shall we talk about today my son?"

Can you think of a greater motivation for taking time to be alone with the Lord than the joy of being with a King who is delighted that you came to see Him and to be with Him?

Chapter Seven

Reverent Submission to His Will and Purposes

Thank you for joining me on this journey of the heart to know and understand something of the King's heart and desires. I hope it has been good for you to study passages that get at answering our key questions: What are the things that are precious to God Almighty our Lord and King? What can we give ourselves to that will bring joy and delight to the King, Jesus our Lord whom we adore? How can we bring a smile our King's heart and cause Him joy?

In previous chapters we've noted that we have become a part of His royal Kingdom right here and now on planet earth. As members of His Kingdom, royal subjects we have been given throne room privileges of prayer in Jesus Christ our Lord and it is very wise for us to spend time with our King in His throne room so that we'll have His individual marching orders for our lives. We reject democratic thought as His subjects and we seek to obey our King wholeheartedly in love. What He asks we give, what He tells we do. Loving gratitude to this King Jesus moves us to want to please Him in lifestyle!

Last chapter we were studying the truth that obedience to God is really precious to Him. We saw that our Father God holds very precious childlike trust and obedience to His commands. In fact when our King gives us a command and we carry it out it is a demonstration of the fact that we live in love to Him, we are His servants and friends. It is the demonstration that the heart of God lives in us; the new heart God alone can create in us. Obedience doesn't change the way God feels toward us. Obedience is an offering of love!

In this chapter of our study we are going to go deeper and look at the in-depth motivations we cherish in our hearts. Studying things that are precious to our King's heart, we now look at a seventh value: **Reverent Submission to His will for our lives** is precious to our King.

I want to again take you into the courtroom of an earthly king as an analogy for our being subjects to our heavenly King. In an earthly kingdom there is a courtroom with a throne in it. On that throne sits a king and around him are gathered his royal subjects. There are warriors and counselors or wise men, there are military advisors and advisors for foreign and domestic affairs. These subjects are all there gathered around their king and if he is a wise king he listens to and weighs very carefully what these people have to say. King Solomon of Israel once wrote, *"In the presence of many counselors there is wisdom."*

But what all of the royal subjects and all of the counselors are there to hear is not what they think but what the king has decided to do. He is the master who holds the authority and as he speaks he sets the direction for the kingdom. Everyone waits to hear what the king has to say and then they swing into action carrying out his decree.

I go to this length to talk about a human king's courtroom to draw an analogy for our individual lives as God's people who are in His Kingdom while we are here on planet earth. What is precious to God our King is when He has a man or a woman whose heart is fully, reverently submitted to His will for their life.

II Chronicles 16:9 *"For the eyes of the Lord range throughout the earth to strengthen those whose hearts are fully committed to Him."*

Of Jesus Christ our Lord it is said in this text, vs. 7 *"During the days of Jesus' life on earth, he offered up prayers and petitions with loud cries and tears to the one who could save Him from death and He was heard because of His reverent submission."*

The word that touches my heart and gives me an insight into what God Almighty my King takes pleasure in is the word - reverent submission, Hebrews 5:7. It is one word in the Greek language – eulabeias – meaning "to esteem in piety, fear, reverence, or circumspection in relation to another." Those definitions draw me to ponder deeply the throne room of the king analogy.

The earthly king is held in reverence and deep respect, fear, anxious to do his will by the royal subjects who surround him. Thus when he speaks it is simply natural for them to respond, "Yes your majesty." An earthly king is sometimes spoken of as "your worship."

Yet as I think about that analogy, and place my life in the context of my desire to serve my King Jesus with all of my heart I find myself coming up woefully short. When I pass my life and my decision making through this grid I see that I have a tendency to make decisions in the natural, using my best data and intelligence, without taking them to God and asking for His wisdom to ask Him what He would like me to do.

And I have to ask myself a really key Christian-life question. Jesus was heard in God's eternal throne room because He chose to come down from heaven to the earth in submission to His Father's will for His life. He never lost sight of the Father's holy majesty and power; He kept hold of His holy fear, held in awe, and absolutely revered His Father. Do I do the same or do I sometimes lose sight of God's majesty? Do I sometimes get so myself so focused or issue centered that I lose sight of His majesty and glory, with the result that concern for God's will isn't center stage anymore?

As our eternal King, the Lord God has a choice, pleasing and perfect will for our lives. He has a plan for us, a heavenly agenda to be accomplished on earth that He is depending on you and me to accomplish.

Some of His will for us is clearly marked out for us in the Scriptures that say " . . . it is God's will for you." All of us are held accountable for this general will of God for all believers: things like; be holy, rejoice, pray, give thanks, be His witnesses, love one another as He loved us.

Some of His will for our lives requires more time and effort on our part. The Lord desires to speak His will into our hearts and lives by His Holy Spirit who lives in us, whispers, impressions, dreams, visions, prophetic utterance, words of wisdom, and by the counsel of respected brothers and sisters. God doesn't leave us as directionless orphans. He wants us to know His will for our lives as much or more than we want to know it.

I find the crucial questions are not in relation to what is God's choice will for my life? Rather the crucial questions are am I reading the Word, fasting and praying, listening to the Holy Spirit's voice to me, and through my brothers and sisters? If His will conflicts with my will am I ready to embrace what God thinks and surrender my will to His will?

The Model of Jesus

Hebrews 5:7 " . . . *He offered up prayers and petitions with loud cries to the One who could save Him from death and He was heard because of His reverent submission.* "

In speaking of His impending death and resurrection, Jesus said in John 14:29 – 31, *"I have told you this now before it happens, so that when it does happen you will believe. I will not speak with you much longer for the prince of this world is coming. He has no hold on me, but the world must learn that I love the Father and that I do exactly what He has commanded me."*

Jesus was completely intimate with the Father. He had left the throne room of glory to take unto Himself humanity to be the sacrifice for the sins of the whole world. Jesus know what brought joy to His Father's heart, what makes the Lord Omnipotent beam with pleasure is reverent submission to His will.

Jesus modeled for us what reverent submission looks like as He walked this planet for 33 years. His agenda was the Father's agenda. He bathed His life in prayer and worship and He went about what the Father wanted Him to do from the very outset of His public ministry. God's will was, for Jesus, the first and the only thing that mattered.

I believe the Hebrew author is making particular reference here in our text to the experience of the Garden of Gethsemane where He made the choice to go to the cross and the statements He made while He died for us on the cross.

In the Garden we're told He prayed in earnest, so intensely that He pours sweat like great drops of blood. He was in agony as He chose to go to the cross and die. His self-preservation gears kicked in and in His humanity He cried over and over "I don't want to this Father God. If you choose to do so you can spare me from this agony of becoming the sin offering of people." I don't think any of us can understand what He was feeling and thinking. The thought of His holiness would actually become sinfulness and His separation from the Father because He bore your sins and mine in His body, had to be absolutely unbearable in His heart. But ultimately it came down to His reverent submission, *"nevertheless not my will, but your will be done."*

Ultimately on the cross Jesus demonstrated holy awe, reverent fear and submission to the Father.

On the cross Jesus bore our sins and in His death made provision for our salvation. He reverently submitted to die for our sins' penalty to purchase our eternal life. On the cross Jesus died to His own will and in the Father's will in reverent submission. But on the cross because of His reverent submission Jesus' death destroys Him who holds the power over death. The devil's power over us is removed for all who believe and receive Jesus Christ and His provisions into our hearts.

The model; the demonstration of Jesus' life demonstrates a spiritual principle for us all. Holy fear, reverent submission brings us to the cross in this life. At the cross we die to our will and live to God's will. The devil's work in us is not destroyed, rendered powerless until we choose to appropriate the power of God in Christ on the cross.

The price has been paid by Jesus Christ for us yet oh how we struggle with our own coming and kneeling at the cross to render ourselves offerings to the Lord for daily living . . . that Jesus might stand tall in our heart and life!

Our King's Work In Us

In the very same way Our Father God by His Spirit was at work in His One and Only Son Jesus, the same Spirit of God is at work in our lives right now. He leads us to long to follow Him, to be after His heart. He permits circumstances to shape us, guides in His paths, and shapes in us the image of Jesus. He does this so that we will learn the significant difference between what is our agenda and what is His will, to teach us to completely, reverently submit to God.

Matthew 4:1 says Jesus *"was led into the wilderness by the Holy Spirit to be tempted by the devil."* God our Father permitted tremendous pain, injustice, and extremely hard experiences into the parameters of His Son's life.

Hebrews 5:8 *"although He was a Son He learned obedience from what He suffered"* are the very next words following the words *"reverent submission."*

It is very clear that in Jesus' life and ministry here on earth what He suffered was permitted by His Eternal Father God to bring Him to a deep place of personal reverent submission, an attitude of loving, worshipful and tender embrace of the Father's holy will for His life, no matter what the cost.

If that was how the Son of God, the One and Only Son learned reverent submission, what about you and me, His adopted sons and daughters? Can we honestly think that we will be immune from suffering in this life? Peter gave us a tremendously honest word in I Peter 4:19. It is a word that we won't hear preached much in our "God wants me to be happy" North American theology. *"So then, those who suffer according to God's will should commit themselves to their faithful Creator and continue to do good."*

I've found that God is intensely interested in bring me to the place of quiet and loving, worshipful and tender embrace of His holy will for my life, no matter the cost. Sometimes He uses tremendously painful circumstances in my life to show me how much flesh and self-interest still remains in me. He is scanning the earth to find a people whose hearts are fully surrendered to Him in holy love to deepen and refine and purify us!

I'd like to give you a little bit different perspective of Romans 8:28. God works all things; people issues that are very hard in our lives or painful circumstances that we just don't know what to do with or where to turn, together for the good of those who love Him, that we might come to the place where we will lay anything and everything at His feet from hearts of loving, tender, reverent submission.

I can easily get my human agenda too high on my priority list and place the will of God, living in reverent submission, holy fear of my Awesome God and King at a lower level than it ought to be. My King is at work in my life to teach me to live at the place of loving, worshipful surrender, to embrace His will for me.

The Cross is the Place of Reverent Submission

Galatians 2:20 *"I have been crucified with Christ and I no longer live, but Christ lives in me. The life I now live in the body, I live by faith in the Son of God who loved me and gave Himself for me."*

I take you back to the actual meaning of our words here in our text rendered *"reverent submission"* in the NIV; it's the word eulabeias and it means, "to hold in awe, great fear, to treat with piety and reverence, anxiety." For Jesus my Lord, embracing the Father's holy and perfect will for His life meant bringing all that He was or ever hoped to be to the cross and dying there. In Jesus Christ my King the cross was the will of God. It was intensely emotional, all consuming, and it cut straight across the grain of His humanity.

Let's get something on the table that must be completely understood. The Kingdom of God could not be established without His reverent submission to embrace the cross. This meant His walking God's holy road to Golgotha in fear and awe of God the Father. This meant laying Himself down on the cross for the cleansing of all who would believe in Him and receive Him as Savior and Lord!

My fellow traveler, the King has not changed. His holy will has not changed and His Kingdom ethic has not changed. The cross of Jesus is still the place of reverent submission for believers in Christ Jesus who would live in His Kingdom here on earth. Everything and everybody who would enter and embrace His holy will for our lives must come through this place of surrender. The kingdom person walks with Jesus and willingly embraces the cross of Jesus!

The cross is intensely personal and emotional. His Kingdom value is complete reverent surrender to His will. The value we have too often embraced in the world is "my way," "autonomy," "I can pull myself up by my own bootstraps." There is an intense conflict in all of our hearts that holy awe, fear, and reverence will conquer given room to germinate and grow!

The cross still requires holy fear, reverence for God to be able and willing to bring all that I am or ever hope to be and by faith put it to death in Jesus' body. I need to be honest, sincere, as in faith I go to the cross and watch the Son of God see Him die for me. His death is my death to my will, desires that conflict with His kingdom and my agenda for my life. It is the test of love in our hearts. The issue is, will we permit the cross to cut straight across our human ways and render us dead to ourselves with Jesus, so that Jesus by His Spirit will stand up tall in us?

Matthew 10:37 – 39 *"Anyone who loves father or mother more than me is not worthy of me; anyone who loves his son or daughter more than me is not worthy of me; and anyone who does not take His cross and follow me is not worthy of me. Whoever finds his life will lost it, and whoever loses his life for my sake will find it."*

Luke 9:23 *"If anyone would come after me he must deny himself and take up his cross daily and follow me."*

Matthew 16:24 – 28 *"Then Jesus said to his disciples, 'If anyone would come after me, he must deny himself and take up his cross and follow me. For whoever wants to save his life will lose it, but whoever loses his life for me will find it. What good will it be for a man if he gains the whole world, yet forfeits his soul? Or what can a man give in exchange for his soul? For the Son of man is going to come in his Father's glory with his angels, and then he will reward each person according to what he has done."*

Whether it is for the very first time or the one hundred first time we are bidden to the cross of our Lord Jesus to put to death what keeps us from reverent submission to His will and purposes for our lives. Will we come to the feet of Jesus and put to death sin, self-interest, and ego needs. Will we reverently, in holy awe and love embrace His will for our lives?

So here is my Hegai counsel to you my fellow traveler on this journey of faith, as we conclude another leg on this journey together. The King beckons you and me to meet with Him in reverent submission at the cross. If we do choose the path of reverent submission, the enemy's control dies at the point of our death to our will, plans, desires and agenda. Anything and everything we surrender at the cross becomes a place where Jesus reigns in us and we are set free to really reign in this life in Christ Jesus! On the other side of the cross, beloved ones, His resurrection power is available to everyone who believes.

Do you hear Him bidding you to the cross and the deep call to reverent submission?

Chapter Eight

The Intercession of His People

I know you know the question by now but let's ask it again. What are the things that are precious, highly esteemed by our King Eternal enthroned in heaven? If we know from His revelation in Scripture what is precious to Him, what our King delights in, we will know what heart attitudes and actions we can embrace to make His heart smile. We'll also know some things we can avoid that will bring Him displeasure too!

The important thing to remember is that the Bible uses kingdom language to describe our relationship to God as His people. He is revealed as King of kings and we are His royal subjects, He is Master and Lord and we are His servants. Remember the picture of the Old Testament kingdom, where the king sat on a throne with a royal scepter in his hand. He held the scepter out to people in the throne room that sought an audience with him. When the king had a special servant whom he felt an affinity towards as a friend, he would always extend the scepter to that person inviting them into intimate conversations.

The truth is Jesus is my King and I am a special and treasured friend to Him. He holds His scepter out to me each and every time I come to His throne of grace to find mercy in my time of need! My King is looking for people whose hearts are fully devoted to His will and purposes for the earth – to publish the beauty of Jesus everywhere!

II Chronicles 16:9 *"For the eyes of the Lord range throughout the whole earth to strengthen those whose hearts are fully committed to Him."*

God has a good, pleasing, and perfect will for our lives and He is intensely interested that we both know His will and carry it out, that in reverence and holy fear we surrender to Him every day, embracing the way of the cross!

In this chapter, we're looking at the eighth thing that is precious, highly esteemed by God: **The Intercessory Prayers offered to Him by His people**. Again I take you to the illustration of an earthly kingdom, the king's palace and his throne room. As you study the eastern kingdoms of the Bible you learn that the king's throne room was a very exclusive place. There were only 2 ways to get into the king's presence; not just anybody could get in to talk to the king or ask something of him.

1) You had to have an invitation.
2) You had to request an audience with him.

I'd like to jog our memory regarding the Bible story of the beautiful young Jewish woman Esther, who became queen of king Xerxes of Persia. A crisis of impending murder of all Jewish people in the empire made it necessary for her to seek an audience with her husband. In Queen Esther's case, she realized by just walking into the presence of the king without an invitation, even though she was his wife, she would be beheaded unless he held out his golden scepter to her bidding her to approach the throne to speak with him.

So Queen Esther fasted and prayed and asked others to fast and pray that she might not die by breaking this protocol of the throne room. When her husband saw her he lit up and welcomed her to the throne, for intimate conversation by holding out the scepter to her.

We have become partakers of the Kingdom of God here and now on planet earth because we have appropriated by faith the finished work of Jesus Christ our Lord in our hearts. We have come to the astounding realization that although weak human beings, subject to failure, because of what Jesus has done for us the scepter of God is always stretched out to us and we may draw near to God, the King Eternal:

Hebrews 4:14 – 16 *"Therefore, since we have a great high priest who has gone through the heavens, Jesus the Son of God, let us hold firmly to the faith we profess. For we do not have high priest who is unable to sympathize with our weaknesses, but we have one who has been tempted in every way, just as we are – yet was without sin. Let us then approach the throne of grace with confidence, so that we may receive mercy and find grace to help us in our time of need."*

Hebrews 10:21 – 23 *"Since we have a great priest over the house of God, let us draw near to God with a sincere heart in full assurance of faith, having our hearts sprinkled to cleanse us from a guilty conscience and having our bodies washed with pure water. Let us hold unswervingly to the hope we profess, for He who promised is faithful."*

There's just no doubt about it, is there? The Scriptures teach us that the avenue of deep and heartfelt prayer is available to every child of God in Christ. We have throne room privileges in the heavenly realms in Christ Jesus. Our text we'll be studying more fully this chapter is Revelation 8:1 – 5. That text teaches us the prayer of God's people is so precious to Him that He stores those prayers in golden bowls and pours them out when He works on the earth. What a tremendous thought!

The Words for Prayer and Intercession:

There are many New Testament words for prayer, words in the Greek New Testament texts that describe different types of prayer or ways we pray in the throne room of God. I Tim. 2:1 is a verse that uses a variety of these different words. *"I urge then, first of all, that requests, prayers, intercessions and thanksgiving be made for everyone . . ."*

a) <u>deesis</u> - "to beg, to request what is lacking." It refers to petition or request for one's personal needs. The word picture is that of a beggar sitting at the side of the road asking help of the King as he passes by. It is "an expression of inadequacy, dependence on another".

b) <u>proseuchas</u> - from two words pros – "by the side of" and euchomai "to wish" want, desire. As it denotes prayers it would be our wishes we express to God on someone else's behalf. It can also refer to our laying our desires beside Him.

c) <u>enteuxeis</u> – whereas in requests and prayers we are concerned for our own needs and desires, in intercession prayer – enteuxeis – we are concerned solely for the needs of others and their best interests before God. Intercession is the unselfish altruistic aspect of prayer. The word enteuxeis means – "to fall in with a person." A word picture would be of a child who goes and asks his daddy for mercy for his little sister who has done wrong.

It is this third type of prayer that is our focus today as another thing that our King Eternal, the Lord Omnipotent delights in. Here God has a servant who loves Him and loves another so much that he or she literally suspends him or herself between God and the other person. The intercessor forgets his or her needs and fully identifies with the needs of the one for whom he or she prays.

There are two classic intercessory prayer passages of the Old Testament. One is the picture of God's friend Abraham suspending himself between God and Lot and Sodom and Gomorrah, and God responded to His man's petition by saving Lot and his family.

The other picture is that of God's intimate friend Moses suspending himself, willing to die if need be, between God and the rebellious people of Israel at the incident of the golden calf. I am touched by what

Moses prayed to God every time I read these words of Exodus 32:31, 32:

"So Moses went back to the Lord and said, 'Oh, what a great sin these people have committed! They have made themselves gods of gold. But now, please forgive their sin – but if not, then blot me out of the book you have written."

The classic New Testament illustration of intercession is our Lord Jesus Christ in John 17 as He, on the eve of His own death, amidst great personal travail and heartache prayed for God's will to be accomplished on earth in His people. Jesus, facing His own impending death by crucifixion, prayed for His disciples to remain true to their calling. He interceded for all of the followers, and that through the establishment of the church their witness would eventually create a place to stand for you and for me!

Why Does God Need Intercession?

Revelation 5:8 *"Each one* (of the 24 elders before the Father's throne) *had a harp and they were holding golden bowls full of incense, which are the prayers of the saints."*

If the intercessory prayer of God's people is precious, highly esteemed and valuable to God, why is it so? Why do we have to intercede? If God is God, He's going to do what He wants to do anyway, so why doesn't He just do it? Why are we in the picture at all; why are the events on earth related to our prayers?

All of us who have prayed know prayer works. There have just been too many unexplainable events and effects of prayer in our daily lives to believe any otherwise. But what really is the purpose of the process of my involvement in prayer and God's work?

In John 5:26, 27 we get a window into the answer to those questions. Jesus said, *"The Father has given Him authority because He is the Son of Man."* One might read that and say it should read that Jesus has authority "because He is the Son of God", but it doesn't say that. It reads *"authority . . . because He is the Son of Man."* It was necessary for Jesus to become the Son of Man that He might take back dominion/authority over the earth from the devil who stole it from mankind.

In the Garden of Eden God placed man in dominion, rule over the earth. But when the man and woman sinned we wrecked, ruined our ability to reign and because of sin now at work in us, Satan controlled the earth. We couldn't even rule ourselves anymore let alone the earth well for God the true King who had given us the authority to do it.

Satan usurped man's authority over the earth through sin and held it until my precious Lord Jesus Christ stepped out of eternity, into humanity, and became the Son of Man to restore dominion to us and free us from the usurper.

Hebrews 2:14 – 16 *"Since the children have flesh and blood, he too shared in their humanity so that by His death He might destroy him who holds the power of death – that is the devil, - and free those who all their lives were held in slavery by their fear of death."*

God had given this authority to rule over the earth to man in the Garden and He does not go back on His Word. What God said would be done must be done. Jesus came in God's image and likeness to create a new family of believers in Him who would exercise the authority and dominion man was created to possess and exert!

Therefore, Jesus came as a man, so that as Son of Man He might triumph over Satan totally. He did this through triumph over Satan's temptation to gain dominion over the earth by worshipping Satan thus leaving Satan still lord of this age. Jesus saw through it and overcame Him there.

It is also true that He became Son of Man in order to His triumph over Satan and all his princes and demons on the cross and in the power of His resurrection to the glory of God the Father. On the cross He overcame the tempter himself forever and ever for all who believe in Him. He openly displayed His victory at Calvary!

Colossians 2:15 *"And having disarmed the powers and authorities, he made a public spectacle of them triumphing over them by the cross."*

What we need to see is that Jesus, Son of Man, redeemed us; paid the price of our sins that we might be forgiven. Jesus restores us as the Last Man to the rightful place of royal sons and daughters, in dominion and authority on the earth, which we lost through the first man.

Romans 5:17 *"For if, by the trespass of the one man, death reigned through that one man, how much more will those who receive God's abundant provision of grace and of the gift of righteousness reign in life through the one man, Jesus Christ."*

Once again, we have the authority to carry out God's will on earth – to bring God's Kingdom to bear on this earth, a kingdom of truth, righteousness, and love. We have that authority in Christ. God has once again committed His authority to rule, have dominion on planet earth to His people; this time it's His church. He wants His will done through our intercession in His throne room! God waits for His people to proclaim His will as His people of authority! "Without Him we cannot; without us He will not"!

Prayers of Intercession Work with God

Revelation 8:3 – 5a *"Another angel, who had a golden censer, came and stood at the altar. He was given much incense to offer, with the prayers of all the saints, on the golden altar before the throne. The smoke of the incense, together with the prayers of the saints went up before God from the angel's hand. Then the angel took the censer, filled it with fire from the altar, and hurled it on the earth;"* . . .

The previous thing we looked at demonstrates why intercession is so important and how the spiritual laws of dominion of the earth committed to man work as we intercede with God. But it's also important to explore why our intercession is so precious to our Omnipotent King Eternal.

God honors the dominion He has given to us and He waits for us to come to Him as His redeemed royal subjects before He will enter the earthly arena. He respects our dominion He delegated to us, that's why He waits for us to come in intercession before He acts. He has committed the proclamation of His will to us.

In effect, the Scriptural truth we're unfolding together is that God will not work on the earth in overriding the collective will of people. He has chosen to voluntarily limit Himself to intercession from His people. He has chosen to position Himself to wait for earnest, sincere, and passionate desire from His people partner with Him, with the result that His will might be done through us. In other words He will not force His way into our world and violate the role of dominion He has committed to us!

E. M. Bounds was a man who wrote a lot about prayer and intercession. He has a quote that comes to mind as I think about this concept of God awaiting our intercession. "Without God we cannot. Without us He will not!" God's people, believers in Jesus Christ, have responsibility in this world that God will not assume, a dominion He will not violate. He longs to be at work and release His power on the earth in the lives of people He loved so much that He sent His One and Only Son to die for them.

Jesus Christ our Lord chose to become one of us to bear away from us our sins and to cleanse us with His own precious blood He shed for us. That is a completed action that has ongoing ramifications for every life on earth that believes and receives Him as Savior and Lord. He bends His ear low to the earth to hear the prayers of intercession of His people, to hear His own suspended between He and another pulling Him to action in that person's life.

Unfortunately what He often hears from those who claim His Name is a "Gimme God" wish-list prayer time that is focused on ours and us. This kind of prayer, which masquerades as intercession is really about what we want and treating the Father as our big prayer Santa Claus in the sky. Sometimes He hears His people pray "at" another person out of frustration, which most of the time has little or nothing to do with genuine faith and submission.

What God is after is a person who will become the embodiment of the burdens in prayer He feels for the lost. He looks for a "Mary-like" heart of intercessory prayer. When God decided to birth Jesus on the earth, He needed a virgin woman's body to become the embodiment of what He was going to do. He found Mary and received an indescribably beautiful response from the teenage girl's heart – *"I am the Lord's servant. May it be to me as you have said."*

He longs for, listens for, but does not often hear a man or a woman in travailing intercession, as a birth channel for His Spirit's dynamic presence moving in their corner of the world praying, "O God, I invite you to come here and now in my city! Do your will Lord in the salvation of thousands in my city and region! Pour out Your Holy Spirit on the earth here and now!"

Intercession Focuses on God's Will

Intercession is prayer we pray that flows out of deepening and intimate relationship with the Lord. Intercession flows out of time alone with

Him in the Word and from "conversations" with Him in fasting and prayer all of which lead us to "discover" God's will. Intercession is asking God to come and do what He wants to do on earth. In this way we become God's *"fellow workers"* as Paul put it in I Corinthians 3:9.

We invite God into our realm of dominion through intercessory prayer that is based on the knowledge of His will. I John 5:14 *"If we ask anything according to His will, he hears us — whatever we ask — we know that we have what we ask of Him."*

I want to return your attention to our verse of Scripture we used as we touched the theme of the reverent submission. Hebrews 5:7 *"He offered up prayers with loud cries and tears to the One who could save Him from death and He was heard because of His reverent submission."* Jesus, as intercessor before God, offered Himself what the Father wanted for His life, including the cross, His death and blood shed there for us. In everything Jesus was about He sought to complete the Father's will on earth! He always refers to and submits to the Father's will.

In the same way the Father depends on Jesus to be the One through whom His will shall be done here on earth. This relationship between the Son and the Father, Jesus depending on the Father for strength by His Spirit, the Father depending on the Son to do His work on earth is a tremendous portrait of what it means for you and for me to be intercessors! Consequently, the Father's greatest power could be at work on the earth at Calvary.

Our intercession requires that we know God, know His will, and that we humbly ask Him to bring His will about on the earth. Our little corner of our world is our God given domain of responsibility and authority. Therefore, the truth remains that God waits for our prayer of intercession before He acts.

When we carry out our authority to pray and intercede, God has the right to come on the scene to display His purpose and His power. Prayer is God's invitation to act in the lives of people we love here on earth! We depend on Him for power to live and intercede and He depends on us to speak authoritatively for Him!

God's man Daniel is forever known by every serious student of Scripture as *"a man highly esteemed by God."* I don't know how those words from Abba God about His man hit you, but that really touches my heart deeply. I ask myself the critical question: Why was Daniel a man highly esteemed by God?

His life gives us our answer as he is portrayed to us in the book that bears his name. He was a man who loved God so deeply that he wanted to please God in what he did or didn't eat, in how he prayed and refused to quit praying under the threat of death, and in tapping into the pain the children of Israel had caused Abba's heart by turning away from Him and following wicked idols. Daniel's prayer life speaks to why God cherished him so much. He prayed until he tapped into the heart of God and what the Lord God had in His heart to do on the earth in and with His people! My heart asks the question: What would the church of Jesus be like and what would our witness on the earth be, if we prayed and interceded until we have touched and been touched by the heart of God?

I want to close this chapter with a word from Dr. Loren Cunningham, Founding Director of YWAM. He points out three things that are happening when we truly intercede before God's Throne of Grace.

1) We pray God's prayers.
2) We feel God's feelings.
3) We'll think God's thoughts.

So here is my concluding Hegai word of exhortation to you, my fellow God-seeker. Intercession before God on behalf of others and the needs they have, is a magnificent privilege. May I ask you a deep, believer's question? Is there anything on earth that could be a better experience than these three things that happen when we intercede for others in the presence of God?

Chapter Nine

"The Worship We Give To Him"

As a member of the holy kingdom of my Lord Jesus, I must ask myself one simple question: What are the things that are precious to this King to whom I declare my love and allegiance? What are the attitudes I may choose to embrace and what actions can I take to bring Him pleasure?

The answer to those questions are all-important, because if we are truly His royal subjects then the obedience question is settled in holy love. Our desire is to please God, honor Jesus Christ our King! We have learned to pray the garden prayer with Jesus: *"nevertheless not my will but your will be done, Father."*

In this chapter we are studying the eighth thing that God esteems, considers to be precious and valuable: Heartfelt, sincere, and meaningful worship. In relation to our public and private worship it is very important that we remember on basic truth: Our Lord Jesus Christ redeemed us and made us members of His church, part of His body for His glory. Jesus ordained and is building the church for Himself! We exist to bring Him glory, spontaneous, and voluntary love!

Therefore, another understanding must follow on the heels of this truth: For God and me to have deepening and intimate relationship, for His heart and my heart to be satisfied with our relationship, I must express the love I feel within me. I must be coming before Him with meaningful, sincere, and heartfelt worship, praise and thanksgiving. The Lord Jesus ordained the church for Himself!

Romans 15:5,6 *"May the God who gives endurance and encouragement give you a spirit of unity among yourselves as you follow Christ Jesus, so that with one heart and mouth you may glorify the God and Father of our Lord Jesus Christ."*

Ephesians 1:11,12 (selected) *"In Him we were also chosen, ...in order that we, who were the first to hope in Christ, might for the praise of His glory."*

I Peter 2:9 *"But you are a chosen people, a royal priesthood, a holy nation, a people belonging to God, that you may declare the praises of Him who called you out of darkness and into His wonderful light."*

The church is in Christ Jesus and the church exists for Christ Jesus. He, therefore, must have the place of prominence and preeminence in our individual lives and in our corporate life. Anything I am doing as a man that does not pass this test of scrutiny of Christ's Lordship in my life must go! And anything in our local church that does not pass this test of scrutiny of His Lordship must go! He must have center-stage in everything:

All eyes focused in faith upon Him ... all adherents gathered around Him and hearts living in love for Him ... and continual praises ascending before Him!

The priority of worship to Christ in the church is certainly not a new thought to us. Every church that is Christian has its packaged phrase in the statement of belief about worship to God the Father, Christ Jesus the Son of God, the Holy Spirit. But what I believe God is challenging us to look at and make a judgment about today is not what we know as truth intellectually. I think He'd like us to honestly answer a much more crucial question; what we are living as reality in our individual daily life? To worship God deeply, meaningfully, and sincerely is to engage in the one thing He wants from you and me: Our love. God desires our love. It is the one thing He has repeatedly asked for from His people throughout salvation history. A simple request from the heart of God: Love Me!

The priority of worship is clearly focused in the Word:

Exodus 20:2,3 *"I am the Lord your God who brought you up out of Egypt, out of the land of slavery. You shall have no other gods before me."*

Deuteronomy 6:4, 5 *"Love the Lord your God with all your heart and with all your soul and with all your strength. These commands that I give you today are to be upon your hearts."*

Hebrews 3:1 *"Therefore holy brothers, who share in our heavenly calling, fix your thoughts on Jesus"*. . . .

Hebrews 12:2 *"Let us fix our eyes on Jesus"*. . .

Hebrews 13:15 *"Through Jesus, let us continually offer to God a sacrifice of praise – the fruit of lips that confess His Name."*

Worship of God in Christ Jesus is the most important thing we do as individuals as families, and as a congregation. Each of us needs to take a long, hard, and fresh look at the satisfaction -- or restlessness and incompleteness of our soul today. For me to be completed from within as a Christian, I need to be regularly touching the heart of God in worship. I cannot be whole or satisfied with my inner life if I am not meaningfully worshipping God. I was created for worship, which in turn inspires and revitalizes me!

II Samuel 22:17 – 21 The MESSAGE *"But he caught me – reached all the way from sky to sea; he pulled me out of that ocean of hate, that enemy chaos, the void in which I was drowning. They hit me when I was down, but God stuck by me. He stood me up on a wide-open field; I stood there saved – surprised to be loved! God made my life complete when I placed all the pieces before him. When I cleaned up my act, he gave me a fresh start."*

There are so many different means we may use in coming to worship Him to express our love to Him. Worship is singing His praises, praising Him with worship for who He is, two-way prayer communion, ministering to His heart and he to mine, offering him thanksgiving for His loving activity, and meditating on His Word to hear His whispers to our hearts

The child of God who comes to God through Jesus Christ our Lord in voluntary, spontaneous, meaningful and heartfelt worship as their first priority of life is experiencing a revolution of the soul, a deep inner transformation which is affecting their whole life! There is no way you can touch the heart of God and have God touch your heart and stay the same. We must change from humanity to Christ-likeness if we are really worshippers! The adverse is also true, if we are staying the same, reverting, or looking back to a time when our spiritual life had more power and we knew a deeper sense of His presence, we probably have not worshipped lately!

II Corinthians 3:16 – 18 *". . .whenever anyone turns to the Lord, the veil is taken away. Now the Lord is the Spirit and where the Spirit of the Lord is there is freedom. And we, who with unveiled faces, all reflect the Lord's glory, are being transformed into His likeness with every-increasing glory, which comes from the Lord who is the Spirit."*

<u>Worship Begins with Desire to Seek the Lord:</u>

The MESSAGE Psalm 40:1 – 5 *"I waited and waited and waited for God. At last he looked; finally he listened. He lifted me out of the ditch, pulled me from deep mud. He stood me up on a solid rock to make sure I wouldn't slip. He taught me the latest God-song, a praise song to our God. More and more people are seeing this: they enter the mystery of abandoning themselves to God. Blessed are you who give yourselves over to God, turn your backs on the world's sure thing, ignore what the world worships;"*

Please notice with me that genuine worship begins with a concrete choice of a loving heart to seek the Lord God personally and deeply. Worship is what happens when we choose to respond to God with eyes of faith and a deep longing of heart to seek the Lord God for who He is: God enthroned and glorious, high and holy, majestic in His splendor, awesome in His presence.

King David has been walking in very hard places in life, lots of pain, as his love song to God points out using the pictures of "the ditch" and "deep mud." Can you relate to feeling as though life has thrown you a pretty tough deal a time or two and you feel like you are in a ditch stuck in deep mud?

But notice what happened in this God-fearing man, King David, as he stayed right at worship, praise and adoration of God regardless of His circumstances. The Lord God reached into his life, touched his soul as he prayed and praised, and David uses the picture of feeling like he was set on a firm solid rock foundation for life. He felt in his heart and soul the renewed love and mercies of God that are new every morning. And at the renewal of his own heart and soul in the mercy and grace of God, look with me at what David says happens in the community of faith.

"He stood me up on a solid rock to make sure I wouldn't slip. He taught me the latest God-song, a praise song to our God. More and more people are seeing this: they enter the mystery of abandoning themselves to God."

This is the only fitting response from a heart that has touched and has been touched by the new mercies of God. Dr Gene Peterson has said it correctly! A life of deep and abiding faith is a journey, a mysterious walk with God that you and I may perhaps have only a faint idea of what He has in mind for us who know Him and love Him. We are invited to adore the Lord God and to enter into the mystery of abandoning ourselves to Him!

This overwhelming sense of the Lord's presence in response to our sincere faith and seeking to know Him is an indispensable element to our understanding of and experience of meaningful worship. David was filled with this kind of awe when he realized that the Lord had in fact acted on his behalf in mercy.

Psalm 40:5, 6 The MESSAGE *"Nothing and no one comes close to you! I start talking about you, telling what I know, and quickly run out of words. Neither numbers nor words account for you."*

In Acts 2 there is a tremendous little clause in verse 43 that is descriptive of the earthly church's worship, *"everyone was filled with awe."* Genuine worship of God is to embrace the heart of a God-Seeker! Jesus told the Samaritan woman He met at the well that the Father God is looking for people who will worship Him with this kind of heart: Spirit and truth flowing from the depths of one's being.

John 4:21 – 24 *"Jesus declared, 'Believe me woman, a time is coming when you will worship the Father neither on this mountain nor in Jerusalem. You Samaritans worship what you do not know; we worship what we do know, for salvation is from the Jews. Yet a time is coming and has now come when the true worshippers will worship the Father in spirit and truth, for they are the kind of worshippers the Father seeks. God is spirit, and his worshippers must worship in spirit and in truth."*

In True Worship I am Conformed to His Image:

The MESSAGE Psalm 40:4 *"Blessed are you who give yourselves over to God, turn your backs on the world's 'sure thing,' ignore what the world worships;"*

The MESSAGE Romans 12:1, 2 *"So here's what I want you to do, God helping you: Take your everyday, ordinary life – your sleeping, eating, going-to-work and walking around life – and place it before God as an offering. Embracing what God does for you is the best thing you can do for him. Don't become so well adjusted to your culture that you fit into it without even thinking. Instead, fix your attention on God. You'll be changed from the inside out. Readily recognize what he wants from you and quickly respond to it. Unlike the culture around you, always dragging you down to its level of immaturity, God brings out the best in you, develops well-informed maturity in you."*

David's love song in Psalm 40 and Paul's word to the Romans are both expounding the same principle: In genuine worship, having been drawn into a personal encounter with the awesome Lord God Almighty, holy and awesome God I am enabled to really see myself clearly in the light of His presence, and some of what I see I am not going to like very much.

Let's be clear with each other that we do not worship with the thought that we are going to get something out of it. We worship with a desire to simply love God, and when we do that, a sidebar benefit is that we are changed more into His image too!

In that classic picture of genuine worship in Isaiah 6, the prophet Isaiah saw the Lord high and holy, lifted up and worshipped by holy beings. When he saw the Lord was shown things in his own life, which displeased God and were clearly not under His holy Lordship which leads me to see a companion truth. Genuine worship of God in His holy presence constrains me to place myself on trial before Him. A revelation of God and of myself is insufficient to bring change unless I am willing to judge myself as having sin and need of life-change. In the Isaiah 6 passage of Scripture, the prophet clearly understood that a deep emotional and spiritual response to God was needed. He willingly prostrated himself before Him in self-examination and personal judgment of his own heart.

When his eyes saw the majesty of God, he then looked at himself and his nation and was deeply moved to confess their corporate guilt, and his own guilt. His overwhelming desire was to be pleasing to the king, clean and usable before Him. He went there with a big problem, to complain about the death of Uzziah, he wound up confessing about Isaiah and the need of his nation.

You may say to me, but Ken, God did all of these adjustments: God moved in Isaiah, God's messenger purged his life, taking the prophet's guilt away. I would say to you, Amen! It is so, but not against his will; the prophet had to cooperate with the seraph and stand still, willing to be cleansed and adjusted!

Yes, God does the work in our lives transforming us from humanity to Christ-likeness when we are meaningfully worshipping but we have to want to be adjusted. This is another voluntary act on our part that is an offering of love for God in our hearts. It proves that we really are His people who dearly love Him and want to bring Him glory on the earth when we hold still while the King prunes His branches.

Beloved brothers and sisters, meaningful, sincere worship from the heart produces the primary affect of adjusting my will to His will; of adjusting my attitude from closed to open to what God wants; and of adjusting thinking from earthly and human to being able to think and perceive from God's perspective. When my will, my attitudes, and my thought-life are being influenced and adjusted then my actions will also of necessity be changed too!

The point is that meaningful, heartfelt, worship of God in Christ Jesus always has a profound effect on my life. I just cannot leave His presence the same as I was when I walked in! Again, back to Acts 2 and the early church profoundly affected by their worship; Luke says they *"ate together with glad and sincere hearts"*: a tremendous picture of the effect of meaningful worship: glad – blessed, exceedingly joyful hearts and sincere hearts – alethia "no stones, no hardness," descriptive of a very open and transparent heart before God!

Genuine worship caused them to be genuine people and that's a kingdom principle and ethic that doesn't change!

Genuine Worship Sends Me into the World as an Instrument:

God Almighty only commissions and sends into the world the genuine worshippers, people who have chosen to be God-seekers and who have been dynamically touched in heart by God.

The MESSAGE Psalm 40:11 – 13 *"But let all who are hunting for you – oh, let them sing and be happy. Let those who know what you're all about tell the world you're great and not quitting. And me? I'm a mess. I'm nothing and have nothing: make something of me. You can do it; You've got what it takes – but God, don't put it off."*

The major truth in this verse that just grabs at the heart of the man with eyes to see it: God commissions and sends people into the world for Him as ministers who are entering into meaningful, personal worship experiences with Him, people who are permitting God's Holy Spirit to have His way in their hearts! The God seekers who are after a deep and personal relationship with Jesus, know the greatness of God and can't help but tell the world He is great and He's not quitting on them anytime soon. The adverse is also probably true. If God is not impassioning us for being an instrument of His love in the world, we are probably not worshipping meaningfully.

When we have truly and deeply worshipped the Lord and when there has been significant life-change take place in us because we have connected with Him from the heart, there is a message of His greatness and glory burning in our hearts. Genuine and heartfelt worship with

God always produces in us a fresh sense of His commissioning of our lives. He adds new fuel and fresh encouragement to the soul of a person who worships Him in Christ.

He makes sure we know, as we minister to Him in worship, He loves us deeply. In the security of being loved by God there is such power to speak His truth! In that passage we saw earlier from the book of Isaiah, the prophet went away from his fresh experience with God, with a burning heart, a commission in his soul that didn't wane regardless of the difficulty of his task.

Isaiah 6:8 *"Then I heard the voice of the Lord saying, "Whom shall I send? And who will go for us?" "And I said, 'Here am I. Send me!'"*

Embracing the Heart of a Worshipper

My Hegai mind is kicking in again, raising all kinds of application questions for you to think about. What do we do with the message of a chapter like this one? How will these thoughts on worship being central to our growth in faith impact the decisions we will make over the next days and weeks? Will I choose to be a private worshiper, telling God audibly how much I love Him?

We can start to respond to it by making a new and fresh commitment of the heart to invest more time alone with God in deep, heartfelt, and fervent worship. I have attempted to help a lot of people in my life in ministry. One of the areas that people often talk to me about is their personal love life with God. It is amazing to me how many people who claim to be followers of our Lord Jesus don't speak aloud their praise and worship of God. It is so important that we speak out to God what we are feeling in our hearts and thinking in our minds. I know the Lord can read our thoughts and knows what we are thinking before we even say it. But the Scriptures are clear that God delights in the sincere praises of His people.

Paul counseled the Roman believers that confessing what we really believe is very important. Paul's words are clear in Romans 10:9, 10 *"That if you confess with your mouth, 'Jesus is Lord,' and believer in your heart that God raised him from the dead, you will be saved. For it is with your heart that you believe and are justified, and it is with your mouth that you confess and are saved."*

There are three people that need to hear you praise and worship the Lord God with all your heart, with all your soul, with all your mind, and with all your strength. These three people are God, because He delights in the praises of His children, and we are commanded to praise Him over and over in Scripture; you need to hear yourself praise Him aloud; and the enemy needs to hear your heartfelt praise and adoration of the Father, because he hates it and moves away from genuine praise and glory given to Jesus! What a great motive for audible praise!

When you gather together with your brothers and sisters in your local church I pray that the following will be true of your worship gatherings. Romans 15:5,6 *"May the God who gives endurance and encouragement give you a spirit of unity among yourselves as you follow Christ Jesus, so that with one heart and mouth you may glorify the God and Father of our Lord Jesus Christ."*

In one of my earlier pastorates, we were experiencing a tremendous move of the Holy Spirit in our Sunday morning worship services. There was a little girl standing in the lobby and she was pulling at her mommy's arm, because she heard the worship music beginning and she wanted to be in her seat to sing to Jesus. Finally in exasperation she said: "Come on mommy wets doe!"

Oh beloved ones, if we all had the hearts of little children to enter into His presence in worship and express ourselves sincerely. "Come on wets doe worship Him!"

Chapter 10

The Death of His People

Our critical question we have been asking and answering is, "What are the things that God delights in, highly esteems, considers to be precious in His sight? If we are truly members of His kingdom of the heart and we know what these things are, then we know some attitudes to cherish and actions to take that will enable us to bring pleasure to the heart of God.

In this kingdom of the heart we have entered there are ethics, values, and transcendent and all-encompassing truths, each of which is based on the delight of the King – Jesus our Lord! For people who live life knowing the Lord the obedience question is settled. The only right answer to any question He asks is "Yes, Lord!"

In this chapter, we turn to the Scriptures to study another thing that is precious to God: the death of His people. Psalm 116:15 *"Precious in the sight of the Lord is the death of his saints."*

We have looked at a number of kingdom principles we have unpacked together in this study. In this chapter we are going to look carefully at another of those kingdom principles in three different ways. **The kingdom principle is: Life through Death**! In the Old Testament God delighted in the smell of burning flesh on the altar because it represented the old covenant worshipper's sorrow for sin, desire to repent of sin, and forsake self-serving ways. In the New Testament God delights in the smell of burning flesh as Christians put to death things in our hearts that prevent us from loving Him more deeply!

The Lord's clear goal, in all of Scripture, has always been that He desires to have us reunite with Him and to enjoy intimate communion with Him. People are God's highest creation and deep love, but sin, the fleshly appetites, our endless pursuit of the worldly, and our self-interest have made deep communion with God a fatal affair. There is a definitive connection in Scripture between our being enabled to see and correctly handle God's glory and the death of our human tendencies to sin, self-interest, and the fame, glamour, and esteem of this world's system of thought!

Moses was a man who got to experience this truth firsthand when he was alone on the mountain with God interceding for the people of Israel who had just committed grievous sin against God with the incident of the golden calf. Exodus 33:18 – 23:

"Then Moses said, 'Show me your glory.' And the Lord said, 'I will cause all my goodness to pass in front of you, and I will proclaim my name, the Lord, in your presence. I will have mercy on whom I will have mercy, and I will have compassion on whom I will have compassion. But,' he said, 'you cannot see my face, for no one may see me and live.' Then the Lord said, 'There is a place near me where you may stand on a rock. When my glory passes by, I will remove my hand and you will see my back; but my face must not be seen.'"

Jesus talked about this principle of life through death in the little parable of the seeds given to His followers in John 12:24 – 26:

"I tell you the truth, unless a kernel of wheat falls to the ground and dies, it remains a single seed. But if it dies, it produces many seeds. The man who loves his life will lose it, while the man who hates his life in this world will keep it for eternal life. Whoever serves me must follow me; and where I am, my servant will also be. My Father will honor the one who serves me."

To walk with the sting of death is to live a life dominated by sin and self-interest and it's accompanying prospect of spending eternity in hell, separated forever from the presence of God and from the ability to have and feel love and grace. There is only one way to have the sting of death removed and that is to lay myself on the altar of God and experience deep and heart-rending brokenness, contrition and humility before the Lord.

In the church of Jesus Christ all over North America we have made the altar a place where we go to stand in line to get some anointed person to pray over us. We seemingly want the altar to be a place of personal blessing; to ask God to "Bless me, Lord," "Touch me, Lord," and "Anoint me for service Lord."

But in the Scriptures the altar is not primarily a place of blessing. It is first and foremost a place of death. Just ask the lamb that was handed to the priest at the altar. It wasn't coming back from the experience the same! But the sweet thing is if we will choose to experience the death the altar of God represents, we will experience the life of God living in our hearts. The New Testament equivalent of death is a voluntary broken, soft, and contrite heart that repents before the Lord of its sinful and selfish ways, a life voluntarily given to Jesus!

The sting of death removed from my life gives me the ability to live as a citizen of heaven while living here on earth. The result is freedom "to live present in the now," enjoying the joy of the Lord in all of the moments I am given now.

Ecclesiastes 5:18 – 20 The MESSAGE *"After looking at the way things are on this earth, here's what I've decided is the best way to live: Take care of yourself, have a good time, and make the most of whatever job you have for as long as God gives you life. And that's about it. That's the human lot. Yes, we should make the most of what God gives, both the bounty and the capacity to enjoy it, accepting what's given and delighting in the work. It's God's gift! God deals out joy in the present, in the now. It's useless to brood over how long we might live."*

Let's take three looks at this principle of life through death, as we think about the death of His people as precious to God – the first two have to do with dying with Christ Jesus now and the third has to do with graduation day.

Death to Sin and the Sin Principle of My Humanity

Romans 6:5 – 8 *"If we have been united with him like this in his death, we will certainly also be united with him in his resurrection. For we know that our old self was crucified with him so that the body of sin might be done away with, that we should no longer be slaves to sin – because anyone who has died has been freed from sin. Now if we died with him we believe that we will also live with him."*

Galatians 2:20 *"I have been crucified with Christ and I no longer live, but Christ lives in me. The life I live in the body, I live by faith in the Son of God, who loved me and gave Himself up for me."*

Paul also wrote in II Corinthians 5:14, 15 *"For Christ's love compels us, because we are convinced that one died for all and therefore all died. And he died for all, that those who live should no longer live for themselves but for him who died for them and was raised again."*

The central message of Christianity finds its true meaning in the simplicity yet profundity of the cross of Christ. The essence of the Christian life is *"Christ in you the hope of glory."* There are two of us living in this one body, and one of us is called to come to the cross daily and die to self! As we come by faith to the cross of Jesus Christ our Lord and see there the sacrifice of love for our sins, His choice to give Himself for us as our redemption price, the way of the cross as the way of love becomes more and more clear.

The one mark of true discipleship to the Lord Jesus Christ is the choice to surrender all that I am, my will, my ways, my prestige and my desires to the Lord! In our culture we have a set of self-centered values that in essence communicate -- "I am my own, that life owes me and I am going to claim all of my rights, do my thing and have my fill." But in the kingdom of God we are bidden to choose to surrender the emptiness of such things as folly and to embrace the message of the cross. The one way to live here and now on planet earth as wholly God's possession is to learn to live by faith in the power of the cross of Jesus our Lord, to go on being crucified with Him there by faith.

The principle of life through death pertains to the sins I have done and the law of sin, that is self-interest that lives in me. In the Old Testament we read stories of how God delighted in the smell of burning flesh, because the burning animal represented the brokenness of God's people for their sins. The truth is that God still today delights in the smell of burning flesh – the more death to self he smells in me, the closer he can come to walk through life with me. God cannot fellowship with human flesh because it reeks of the world's values. What the Lord is after is dead flesh, crucified and purified in the precious blood of Jesus.

In passage cited earlier from Exodus 33:17 – 20, when Moses asked to see God's glory the Lord's response to him was profound. *"You cannot see my face; for no one can see me and live."* If we behold God for who He is and His glorious presence is manifested to us there will be a death of something of our humanity, our self and self-interest.

The Apostle Paul says in I Corinthians 1:29 KJV *"That no flesh shall glory in His presence."* It can't because it stinks to God and it must be burned up by holy fire of His love for us! God's resurrection power is only poured out on those who know the power of His crucifixion in our lives daily. God doesn't pour Himself into those of us who are full of our life, our will, and our desires. There is a significant connection between His glory and our death. Resurrections are only found in graveyards, where someone has died.

Jesus said Luke 9:23, *"If any one would come after me, he must deny himself and take up his cross daily and follow me."*

The Lord's goal is reunion and communion. For those two things to happen; our reuniting with the Lord God and walking with Him through life in intimate communion and fellowship, sin and self-interest cannot be permitted to reign in our lives. Sin and self-interest must be dealt with by faith with Jesus at the cross, each new day!

Romans 6:11 – 14 *"In the same way, count yourselves dead to sin, but alive to God in Christ Jesus. Therefore do not let sin reign in your mortal body so that you obey its evil desires. Do not offer the parts of your body to sin, as instruments of wickedness, but rather offer yourselves to God, as those who have been brought from death to life; and offer the parts of your body to him as instruments of righteousness. For sin shall not be your master, because you are not under law, but under grace."*

Death to the World and It's Allure to My Self-Interest

Galatians 6:14 *"May I never boast except in the cross of our Lord Jesus Christ, through which the world has been crucified to me, and I to the world."*

Why is the world system of things so reprehensible to God? Why would the Lord tell us to live life crucified to the world and the world crucified to us? The truth is that the world system of things in which we live, is the complete and diametric opposite of the values and ethics of the kingdom of heaven.

Mark Bubeck in his book "The Adversary" defines the world system as, "The value system in its function is a composite expression of the depravity of mankind and the intrigues of Satan's rule, combining in opposition to the Sovereign rule of God." I absolutely love this brother's definition.

The world system of things teaches us to place self at the center of life and to be materialistic and consumer-based in our thinking. The world's way of thinking is to ask the simple question: "What's in it for me?" The value system is that the only thing that matters is that you get to the top of the heap, that you have everything you think you want to make yourself happy.

The world system says finding the person of your destiny is the goal of life. He/she will make you happy. The kingdom of God's value is that you and I are responsible to be the right kind of person. Happiness is a matter of the heart attitude.

The world system says having many things, status, and prestige make you more valuable as a person. The kingdom of God's value is that when you love, give of yourself, and choose to serve it adds value to your soul.

The Lord makes it painfully clear in Scripture that very often our human ways and our human reason, based upon our knowledge and experiences of life, often interfere with our seeking to know and understand Him and His ways for us. How often we meet people, in stories in the Bible, that just couldn't get at what the Lord was trying to teach them about Himself, because their own prejudices and presuppositions.

The ways and the stuff of this world can be, and very often is, a detriment to really hungering and thirsting to know God. Time and attention can be and very often are diverted away from the things of life that really matter by the screaming and clamor for attention by the stuff of this life.

Death to self-interest, to selfishness and the allure of this world system of values to my fleshly nature, is freedom from the grip of the material and earthly, and freedom to seek a deeper walk with God each new day. The principle of life through death as it relates to the world system is a powerful principle of being enabled to really enjoy life. Death to the world and the values that accompany it permits me to experience and value true riches of heaven, and gives me the ability to enjoy them now!

The Lord's goal is reunion and communion and for those two things to happen we must choose to live crucified to the world and the values of the world system in which we live. What the Lord desires is that we put to death the ways of this world because we cannot embrace the world order of things and walk intimately with God.

The Death of His People – Entering Into His Presence

Psalm 116:5 – 8 *"The Lord is gracious and righteous; our God is full of compassion. The Lord protects the simplehearted; when I was in great need, he saved me. Be at rest once more, O my soul, for the Lord has been good to you. For you, O Lord, have delivered my soul from death, my eyes from tears, my feet from stumbling, that I may walk before the Lord in the land of the living."*

Psalm 116:15, 16 *"Precious in the sight of the Lord is the death of his saints. O Lord, truly I am your servant, the son of your maidservant; you have freed me from my chains."*

Remember the kingdom principle we have been thinking about today is the principle of life through death – and the truth is that death is something we will all experience, unless the Lord steps into the earth and takes us out of here. Death is not the end of life; it's a doorway. When we die we go to sleep down here but we awaken there!

Out of all of God's creation He has given human beings the ability to know and prepare for our impending death. Every person, in honest and unguarded moments, knows he/she is going to die sooner or later. And beyond that He has given us His One and Only Son as a sin offering to remove the sting of death, the threat of eternal punishment for all who have believed in Him and receive Him as Savior and Lord!

There are people who have gone before me that have entered into what I at present can only imagine, based on what Scripture teaches me. I know that the Bible teaches me that my loved ones are in paradise with Jesus. I know that they know Him personally, deeply, and that they know each other. And I know that because I am God's son in Christ Jesus I will join them in His presence!

The principle of life through death teaches us to embrace heaven, being in the very presence of God, as our true home, and to think about this life as simply a transient existence until real life begins. This life is about getting us ready for the next one! A person who lives with a kingdom heart is always moving a little closer to his real and true home with each passing day. This mindset enables us to see our lives, our selves, and material things in a whole different light.

Jim Elliot who was martyred by the Auca Indians wrote: "He is no fool who gives up what he cannot keep to gain what he cannot lose." That is a nice platitude, and it sounds so good and so right. It is written on placards that grace many walls of Christian businesspersons' offices and people's homes. It is a lot harder to believe when it comes time to live it out personally!

The Hebrew author wrote about this in Hebrews 11:13 – 16 *"All these people were still living by faith when they died. They did not receive the things promised; they only saw them and welcomed them from a distance. And they admitted that they were aliens and strangers on earth. People who say such things show that they are looking for a country of their own. If they had been thinking of the country they had left, they would have had opportunity to return. Instead, they were longing for a better country – a heavenly one. Therefore God is not ashamed to call be called their God, for he has prepared a city for them."*

Peter wrote about this in I Peter 2:11: *"Dear friends, I urge you, as aliens and strangers in the world, to abstain from sinful desires, which war against your soul."*

The Lord's goal is reunion and communion. He has prepared us for death – consummation day! He is waiting for us at the finish line of this marathon race we call life. He has a word for all who run to the tape – "Well done good and faithful servant. Enter you Master's happiness!"

So my Hegai heart of love for you is kicking in again, as we close this chapter. In my city we have great chapter of the Salvation Army. Their signboard this week said: "Live today like you will stand before God tomorrow!" I like the word I read in an article addressing true life recently, "Make sure you live so well that when it comes time to die all you have to do is die!" My Hegai counsel to you is, in the words of Tim McGraw's song – "Live like you were dying," because truthfully, we all are, and it's not the end of life for the child of God, it's rather a doorway to reunion and communion!

Chapter Eleven

Living in the Mercy of God

We have been looking at the Scriptures to ask and answer this crucial question: What are the things that are valued, highly esteemed, and precious to God? The reason for asking that question is very simple. If we know from His Word what is precious to God and we are His royal subjects, then we will know what must also become highly valued to us. In the kingdom of the heart, we have entered into by faith in Jesus, there inherent ethics, values, and transcendent and all-encompassing truths, each of which is based on the delight of the King – Jesus our Lord.

Living in God's Kingdom on earth is about walking in fellowship with God because our sins are all pardoned and our guilt is removed. The central issue is knowing Jesus personally and deeply. John the Baptist had it right when he shared two incredibly important words with us about what it means to know the Lord Jesus.

John1:29 *"Behold the Lamb of God who takes away the sin of the world!"*

John 3:29, 30 *"The bride belongs to the bridegroom. The friend who attends the bridegroom waits and listens for him, and is full of joy when he hears the bridegroom's voice. That joy is mine, and it is now complete. He must become greater; I must become less."*

We have also noted in previous chapters that embracing the kingdom of God in our hearts means deciding to love what God loves. That choice invariably puts us squarely at odds with the cultural values of the world system in which we live. We've noted that our cultural setting, the conditioning of our ears is America and democratic process, we value our individualism and our personal freedoms. The language of Scripture is Kingdom language in which God in Christ Jesus is King and we are His servants, and this out of our love. Our ears and hearts must hear His words of instruction and command as loving subjects and that we are called to live out our faith walk with the Lord in community with our brothers and sisters.

In this chapter we are studying our tenth thing that is precious to God: **Living in His mercy**. There are two texts from which we are taking the themes addressed in the message today.

Micah 7:18, 19 *"Who is a God like you, who pardons sin and forgives the transgression of the remnant of his inheritance? You do not stay angry forever but **delight to show mercy**. You will again have compassion on us; you will tread out our sins underfoot and hurl all our iniquities into the depths of the sea."*

James 2:12, 13 *"Speak and act as those who are going to be judged by the law that gives freedom, because judgment without mercy will be shown to anyone who has not been merciful. Mercy triumphs over judgment!"*

As we turn our thoughts to the topic, I'd like us to begin with serious personal reflection on the following questions. When you think about a mental picture of God, what do you see? Do you see Him as a God of justice? Is He angry at sin and ready to pounce on you for every mistake you make? Or do you see Him as a God who loves us so much He offers us mercy and kindness just as we are, and loves us too much to allow us to stay the way we are living?

What kind of throne is He presently sitting on? Is God presently sitting on a Throne of Judgment, is He angry at us and coming to destroy His enemies? Is He sitting on a Throne of Grace from which He desires to dispense mercy to us because He is compassionate, gracious, rich in love, and forgiving of sins we have committed?

In this chapter we are studying another kingdom principle: Mercy triumphs over judgment, found in James 2:13b. God came after humankind with severe and tender mercy in His heart and chose not to give us what our sins deserve. In His wrath against our sins and our sinfulness, He remembered mercy.

--Mercy is – compassionate pity aroused by the distress of another, rather than severe behaviors toward someone who is in one's power.

--Grace is – the underserved favor of God that is poured into our hearts freely in Christ Jesus our Lord. Francis Frangipane wrote of grace: Grace is God's power, motivated by His mercy, working to fulfill His compassion."

--Judgment is – to hear a case and render a decision on the basis of applied laws, to examine and determine either merits or punishment deserved.

As God looked down on us, even before we were born, I am so grateful He chose to give us mercy instead of justice. I am so thankful that His heart of mercy triumphed over judgment of our lives in and through Jesus Christ our Lord. The mercy of God was revealed to our hearts long before we believed in His grace or received Him as Savior. Mercy opened the door of our hearts to be able to receive and experience deep levels of His grace.

Mercy Poured Into Our Hearts

Micah 7:18 – 20 *"Who is a God like you, who pardons sin and forgives the transgression of the remnant of his inheritance? You do not stay angry forever but delight to show mercy. You will again have*

*compassion on us; you will tread out our sins underfoot and hurl all
our iniquities into the depths of the sea."*

Habakkuk 3:2 *"Lord, I have heard of your fame; I stand in awe of your
deeds, O Lord, Renew them in our day, in our time make them known;
in wrath remember mercy."*

We simply must understand that God has predisposed Himself to be
merciful to you and me. We have been given access to the Mercy Seat
of God, access into the presence of the king. Remember the Old
Testament picture of the king sitting on his throne, with a golden
scepter in his right hand? There were only two ways to legally approach
the throne of an earthly monarch.

    a. One – you had to have been invited to show up, to have an
       audience with the king.

    b. Two – when you walked into the courtroom the king could
       extend to you the scepter in his right hand granting you the
       ability to approach him and converse with him.

The awesome good news of the Bible is that our King Jesus has made
the Throne of Grace available to us all. Our King is always glad to see
us and the scepter of His grace is always extended to us.

The mercy of God extended to us moves Him to bring two tremendous
gifts of grace to us in accepting us and adopting us as sons and
daughters: His love and His forgiveness for us. And please understand
this love for us is while we are yet sinners and His forgiveness of us, is
absolute. In the word in Micah 7:18 and 19 God told them He was
washing away their sins committed, iniquitous patterns, and their
unintentional transgressions. That pretty much runs the gamut!

Please go deeper than just perceiving His mercy producing love and
forgiveness of us. Go farther on the path of mercy with God and see the

view of sin Jesus had from the cross. All sin and sinful patterns in our lives, and His forgiveness of them, must be viewed through the lenses of the cross, the body of Jesus ripped and torn apart bearing in Himself all of our sins – even those we'd deem to be lesser. At the cross the view of Jesus regarding sin and forgiveness is a severe mercy. It deals with sin and with sin's power. It moves the Lord to take our place! At the cross of Jesus, justice exacted on sin in people by having the body of the Son of God actually become guilty for those things.

II Corinthians 5:21 *"God made him who had no sin to be sin for us, so that in him we might become the righteousness of God."*

What we all so desperately need is to experience the view of God's judgment of sin and its punishment from the cross. At the cross we see incredibly severe mercy. The wrath of God is poured into Jesus, in judgment of our sins, as well as our propensity or leaning to sin, our fleshly behaviors that are just full of self-interest, is poured out on His One and Only Son Jesus!

Isaiah 53:4, 5 and 10 *"Surely he took up our infirmities and carried our sorrows, yet we considered him stricken by God, smitten and afflicted. But he was pierced for our transgressions, he was crushed for our iniquities; the punishment that brought us peace was upon him, and by his wounds we are healed. ... Yet is was the Lord's will to crush him and cause him to suffer, and though the Lord makes his life a guilt offering, he will see his offspring and prolong his days, and the will of the Lord will prosper in his hand."*

Mercy In Our Speech and Actions:

James 2:12 *"Speak and act as those who are going to be judged by the law that gives freedom."*

James was teaching the people of God about the issue of having received mercy deeply in our hearts and lives. He tells us how to conduct ourselves in our interpersonal relationships. He exhorted them to speak and act as people who have experienced the law of grace and peace with God that brings freedom, not bondage to the human heart. In order to treat others in this way we must choose to cherish the experience of His mercy deeply in our hearts and lives. We just cannot lose sight of this incredible truth in our hearts that at the cross of Jesus Christ our Lord His mercy flowed to us while we were yet sinners. We got His mercy, compassion, and pity poured into our hearts.

If we are to choose to treat others with mercy and grace, as those who will be judged by the law of love that gives freedom, we need to know how badly we need His mercy. Too often, we tend to think our sins weren't that bad, and we lose sight of what our sins cost the Lord Jesus. We tend to categorize sins, that things like murder, adultery, and other forms of immorality are much worse than other sins that are little sins.

That is a human view of sin and its consequences that has to go. The fact of the matter is that as God views sins, He categorizes slander, gossip, and jealousy in the same grouping as murder, adultery, and witchcraft. Galatians chapter five is a catalogue of sins of the flesh that God says, shall not inherit the kingdom. You will find the "little sins," according to human thinking, in the same list as the ones we might deem "big sins." The fact is that none of us got what we deserved at the cross of Jesus. He took what we deserved!

Our job is to understand a very simple principle of life: What we cherish in our hearts today will become our words and deeds tomorrow. Jesus said it this way in Matthew 12 *"Out of the abundance of the heart the mouth speaks."* Today's attitudes become tomorrow's actions. God delights to give us mercy and He delights when we give mercy to others. So if we are speaking with each other in ways that point fingers, speaking words of judgment and criticism, we are speaking from a lack of His mercy cherished as a value in our hearts.

In the Scripture there is a law of sowing and reaping. This is not telling us that we get what is coming to us, or retribution in life that is justice-based. It is a law of mercy. What you have received from God and give to each other you get more of in your own life. Show me a person who is merciful to the people in his or her world and I will show you a person who has been spending time in the heart of God cultivating His mercy. Our human and natural tendency towards self-interest in our lives means that in our relationships with others we definitely do not lean towards being merciful!

James 2:13a *"...because judgment without mercy will be shown to anyone who has not been merciful."*

Matthew 7:1 – 5 *"Do not judge, or you too will be judged. For in the same way you judge others, you will be judged, and with the measure you use, it will be measured to you. Why do you look at the speck of sawdust in your brother's eye and pay no attention to the plank in your own eye? How can you say to your brother, Let me take the speck out of your eye, when all the time there is a plank in your own eye? You hypocrite, first take the plank out of your own eye, and then you will see clearly to remove the speck from your brother's eye."*

I can only speak for myself. I need a tremendous amount of mercy in my life, so I have made a decision of the heart. I have decided, since I have received the tender mercy of God, His compassionate pity for me in my helplessness, I want to be a man of mercy with people. I have decided that I want to err on the side of mercy, not on the side of judgment. I don't honestly believe they will think mercy from me is condoning their sins.

If I understand the law of sowing and reaping properly, then I must believe mercy from me will pave the way for people to receive it from Him. They'll want to know why I care and why don't speak condemnation. When they ask I'll tell them about what I've received and leave the convicting to His Spirit as he works in them!

Jesus said in Matthew 7:12, *"So in everything, do to others what you would have them do to you, for this sums up the law and the prophets."* Generally speaking people know they have sins in their hearts and lives, but they don't know God loves them and is merciful toward them, despite their sins. They need to experience His mercy before they'll be able to hear His message of grace, the forgiveness of sins through Jesus' sacrifice on the cross. They need to experience mercy from people. If people can't see a concept in their minds it is unlikely they will understand it.

Galatians 6:7 – 10 *"Do not be deceived: God cannot be mocked. A man reaps what he sows. The one who sows to please his sinful nature, from that nature will reap destruction; the one who sows to please the Spirit, from the Spirit will reap eternal life. Let us not become weary in doing good, for at the proper time we will reap a harvest if we do not give up. Therefore, as we have opportunity, let us do good to all people, especially to those who belong to the family of believers."*

Paul's words encourage the readers to go on sowing to please the Holy Spirit. Give away what we have so graciously been given by God! The promise is that we will definitely reap a harvest that's blessed by the Holy Spirit, if we don't quit sowing!

Mercy Triumphs Over Judgment:

The place where we need to stand as we give mercy to people is to remember just how much we have received from the Lord. When the Lord came looking for us He did so in drawing mercy and love. His mercy caused Him to come down from heaven and walk among us, to show us what God is like, in human terms we could understand. He talked to us about a father looking down the road waiting for his erring son to come home. Then Jesus went on to mount a cross and shed His blood to satisfy justice on our behalf. Our merciful God took into Himself everything you and I had ever done that was offensive to Him, and destroyed it in His body, dying the death our sins, transgressions, offenses against God's holiness, and iniquitous patterns deserved!

When we understand this and choose to go deeper into His heart of mercy and grace – we are gripped by the fact, that mercy triumphs over judgment, in my life and then for the people with whom I live, mercy triumphs over judgment.

In the Kingdom of God dwelling in the human heart, we are commanded to give away to others what we have received from the Lord and when we do, more will be given to us! Listen to the words of Jesus which are in the context of what we sow in our human relationships, Luke 6:37, 38 *"Do not judge, and you will not be judged. Do not condemn, and you will not be condemned. Forgive, and you will be forgiven. Give and it will be given to you. A good measure, pressed down, shaken together, and running over, will be poured into your lap. For with the measure you use, it will be measured to you."*

The Lord Jesus comes at this thing from a bit different angle but He says the same thing. If we are being hard on each other's faults, and running in unending cycles of needing to fix people, we do not understand His kingdom well. If we are being hard on each other God will increase the standard by which we will be judged.

What He is after is our choice to embrace the truth that in my life and yours mercy has triumphed over judgment. What I have been so freely given I am responsible to give to everyone in my life. There are many people in my life who need to experience the precious mercy of God. If they are going to experience mercy from God's heart they will have to see it first in me. They need a picture of what mercy is and does.

Here's Hegai talking again. How about you and me as we interact with people in our lives? Are you known as a man or woman of compassion, that people want to talk to because they know you will care and show them mercy? What trail are you leaving behind you in the lives of others? Is mercy triumphing over judgment in your heart? How about in your relationships with people in your sphere of influence? Mercy from the heart of God has burst into your heart setting you free from sin and self-interest. That same mercy that has so radically changed you and me must flow out of us to our loved ones today. So let's get on with glorifying this King Jesus. Let's speak to one another from hearts that are overwhelmed by what He has done to make the mercy of God available to us and to the lost in our sphere of influence!

Chapter Twelve

"The Precious Cornerstone"

Throughout this book we've been seeking to answer a question that is crucial for God's people to consider as people who have entered the Kingdom of God on earth. What are the things that are precious, highly esteemed by our King Eternal enthroned in heaven?

In the introduction to the book I used an illustration from the life of Esther and Xerxes, a picture drawn from natural love to illustrate spiritual verities. Before she became Queen, the beautiful maiden Esther spent an entire year in beauty treatments under the supervision of a man who intimately knew the likes and tastes of King Xerxes. Esther gave herself to those things that the king delighted in. She wore his favorite fragrances, ate his favorite foods, and wore his favorite fabrics. She immersed herself in making herself look beautiful to the king and the king only. What a great picture of what our Christian life can and should be characterized by: Giving ourselves to those things that make us more delightful to our King.

If we know from His revelation in Scripture what is precious to Him we will know what heart attitudes and actions we can embrace to make His heart smile and be filled with joy. We'll also know some things we can avoid that will bring Him displeasure!

It's important to remember that the Bible uses kingdom language to describe our relationship to God as His people. He is revealed as King of kings and we are His royal subjects; He's Master and Lord and we are His servants. We have been raised in an environment that doesn't hear kingdom language and motif well. But the truth is that when we turn to the Lord and believe in Him as Savior and Lord, we have embraced something that is far bigger than we are, and the Lord God who is awesome and majestic now lives in our hearts, by His Holy Spirit.

We deepen our journey through the things that God esteems with another amazing thing God delights Himself in: God the Father is delighted in His Son and our Savior, **Jesus the Precious Cornerstone**. When you and I come to the end of ourselves, see our need of a Savior, repent of our sins, open our hearts to believe and receive Jesus into our hearts, we choose to build our lives on the firm foundation of God's salvation. Jesus becomes our personal precious cornerstone!

I Peter 2:4 – 6 *"As you come to him, the living Stone – rejected by men but chosen by God and precious to him – you also like living stones, are being built into a spiritual house to be a holy priesthood, offering spiritual sacrifices acceptable to God through Jesus Christ. For in Scripture it says: 'See, I lay in Zion a chosen and precious cornerstone, and the one who trusts in him will never be put to shame."*

Peter's words are nearly a verbatim quote of Isaiah 28:16, which says; *"See, I lay a stone in Zion, a tested stone, a precious cornerstone for a sure foundation; the one who trusts will never be dismayed."*

Paul expounds the very same truth in the powerful picture he paints of building our lives on Jesus in Ephesians 2:19 – 22. *"Consequently, you are no longer foreigners and aliens, but fellow citizens with God's people and members of God's household, built on the foundation of the apostles and prophets, with Christ Jesus himself as the chief cornerstone. In him the whole building is joined together and rises to become a holy temple in the Lord. And in him you too are being built together to become a dwelling in which God lives by his Spirit."*

The Scriptures are giving us a building metaphor that is important for us to see and understand. **No building is stronger than its foundation**. The cornerstone laid in the foundation was the unifying piece, the place of stability for that building. A celebrity often laid it at a grand ceremony. As anyone who has ever worked on any building project with me will tell you I am not a carpenter. My style of construction could best be referred to as wood-butcher. But I am responsible to be another kind of builder, so I must understand this picture and make application of it.

I am responsible to build a personal life that works for the glory of Jesus my Savior each day in the way I live with my wife, my family, you as my church family, and in my community.

And I am responsible to build up the lives of others in our church family together with you. I'm responsible to make disciples and teach what He says and thinks, that we may do the best we can to help each other grow in our experience of His salvation.

And like you, I am responsible to build the kingdom of God on earth in my little corner of the world, to want to help people who don't know Jesus yet to come to know Him personally and deeply.

The key questions of life put forth to each of us by this Biblical metaphor: What am I building? And what am I building it on? This really isn't rocket science. All we have to do is look at the wake our lives have cut in the water and it will be very clear to us what we are building and what or whom we are building it on. What footprint is my life leaving in the lives of people with whom I live? Is it one of investment and grace or is it self-focus and agendas?

The world system is selling you the foundation of the material world of riches and goods in the here and now. Throughout this series we've noted that our culture values consumerism, the love of and being enamored with the outward and the material. As His subjects in His kingdom here on earth we must choose to cherish what God values and that will often cause us to cut straight across the grain of our culture, and sometimes be very much misunderstood.

Romans 12:1, 2 The MSG *"So here's what I want you to do, God helping you: Take your everyday, ordinary life – your sleeping, eating, going-to-work and walking around life – and place it before God as an offering. Embracing what God does for you is the best thing you can do for him. Don't become so well adjusted to your culture that you fit into it without even thinking. Instead, fix your attention on God. You'll be changed from the inside out. Readily recognize what he wants from you and quickly respond to it. Unlike the culture around you, always dragging you down to its level of immaturity, God brings out the best in you, develops well-informed maturity in you."*

The kingdom of God in the heart teaches us to build our lives on something that is permanent, something that is sure and lasting, rather than the foolishness of building on the here and now, as though this is all there is to life! The Bible is clear: God cries out to us all, please don't build on something that is so temporary. I John 2:17 *"The world and its desires pass away, but the person who does the will of God lives forever."*

We are called to drink living water from **the River of God's Delights**!

Psalm 36:7, 8 *"How priceless is your unfailing love! Both high and low among men find refuge in the shadow of your wings. They feast on the abundance of your house; you give them drink from your river of delights."*

John 7:37 – 39 *"On the last and greatest day of the Feast, Jesus stood and said in a loud voice, 'If anyone is thirsty, let him come to me and drink. Whoever believers in me, as the Scripture has said, streams of living water will flow from within him. By this he meant the Spirit, whom those who believed in him were later to receive.'"*

John the Baptist was a man who understood where real life is found and how a life of meaning and grace can be lived. It is to his life that I sensed the Lord lead me to pull out three wonderful principles concerning how you and I can walk through life building on Jesus the Chief Cornerstone – He who holds our life together when everything seems to be coming apart!

Behold the Lamb of God

John 1:29 *"The next day John saw Jesus, coming toward him and said, 'Look, the Lamb of God who takes away the sin of the world!'"*

The Gospel of John clearly gives us the setting of these startling and powerful words. John the Baptist is at the height of his prophetic preaching ministry. He has a significant number of personal followers or disciples who can clearly see that God is at work in John's heart and life. He has been calling people who have been going through religious motions to come back to God in deep, heartfelt, and personal repentance of their sins. He has been baptizing repentant sinners in the Jordan River, preparing them for the coming kingdom of God.

The religious leaders of the day were pretty upset by John's words that condemned outward religious pretense with no passion for God. In Matthew 3:7 – 10 in essence he called them a bunch of snakes, whose status quo message of same-old, same-old go through the outward motions, with no heart in it, no dynamic of life-change at all, was actually turning people away from the kingdom of God not bringing them into it.

John was preaching to Jewish people, to people who knew the Biblical story of the Passover lamb of sacrifice. But the truth of what the Passover really represented was being completely missed. They were making it about deliverance from Egypt, a nationalistic holiday of deliverance from slavery to the Egyptians and to the freedom of the Promised Land.

John's cry, *"Behold the Lamb of God who takes away the sin of the world,"* harkens back to the Passover Lamb of sacrifice, but this time with the truth of what God was trying to bring to them when He instilled the Passover. Yes, you were delivered from Egypt and into the Promised Land. But what it represents is a much greater deliverance than from foreign oppression and into the freedom of your new land.

What the Passover Lamb represents is deliverance from the slavery to sin and sin's power, slavery to endless self-interest. We are delivered from the tyranny of valuing what this world system is enamored with – pride, ego wrapped up in outward trappings of success, and materialism. We are delivered ultimately from slavery to the enemy of our souls Satan. And we are set free to know the Lord God in and through the Spirit of Jesus living in our lives, freedom to love God and people, freedom to serve God with joy and gladness.

Here is what each of us is called to see and understand about what we are building and what we are building it on. Being set free from sin and given the ability to serve God is absolutely an issue of entering into what Jesus Christ our Lord has already done for us. Behold the Lamb of God. See Him for who He is and hold fast to Him because of what He has done.

He's the One who has taken away our sins, crucified them, and destroyed them for all of us who've believed and received Him as Savior and Lord. He has set us free from sin to know the Lord God as sons and daughters, and to serve the Lord with joy in our hearts! He has taken up residence in our hearts and lives by His Spirit, pouring His life into our lives because we have responded to Him by faith.

The Source of True Joy

John 3:27 – 29 *"To this John replied, 'A man can receive only what is given him from heaven. You yourselves can testify that I said, 'I am not the Christ but am sent ahead of him.' The bride belongs to the bridegroom. The friend who attends the bridegroom waits and listens for him, and is full of joy when he hears the bridegroom's voice. That joy is mine, and it is now complete."*

There is a powerful principle about inner joy and satisfaction that John pours out of his heart for all who have eyes to see and ears to hear. The principle is: The inner joy of living for something that is greater than you. In this particular case John is talking about himself living with a heart for God's kingdom, for the honor and the glory of Jesus.

The picture John uses to describe what a kingdom heart looks like is the picture of the friend of the bridegroom – in today's vernacular "The Best Man." When the best man accpts the position as the bridegroom's dear friend, he does so understanding that his role is simple. He is responsible to serve the groom and to do everything he can to make the bride and the groom's wedding day a special occasion.

John uses terminology that is compelling, *"The bride belongs to the bridegroom. The friend who attends the bridegroom waits and listens for him, and is full of joy when he hears the bridegroom's voice."* In those days the wedding ceremony was essentially a two-family party that went on for many days. Finally, at the consummation of the event, there was a shout, usually at night. The best man escorted the bridegroom to the bedroom of the bride. He took her in his arms and swept her off to their new home. There was tremendous joy at the procession from her father's home to her new home as wife of her bridegroom.

John says, his role with the Lord Jesus and the preaching he has been doing is really pretty basic. He says the joy in his heart to see people following Jesus is like the best man who hears the shout and sees the emergence of his friend the bridegroom. He sees the joy and delight on his friend's face at the prospect of holding his bride in his arms on their wedding night.

John concludes with these powerful words, *"The friend who attends the bridegroom waits and listens for him, and is full of joy when he hears the bridegroom's voice. That joy is mine, and it is now complete."*

This is what it is like to be a person who has chosen to be a follower of Jesus. It is a matter of first and foremost being His friend, learning to know His heart, and listening for His voice of direction.

John 15:14, 15 *"You are my friends if you do what I command. I no longer call you servants, because a servant does not know his master's business. Instead, I have called you friends, for everything that I learned from my Father I have made known to you."*

John 10:27 *"My sheep listen to my voice; I know them and they follow me."*

Deep and profound inner joy is a matter of choosing to live for something greater than yourself. Joy in the soul is found when we know Him as Savior and Lord, hear His voice of direction, and then choose to live in such a way as to be able to point people to see Him, to behold the Lamb of God who takes away the sin of the world.

Building my life on Jesus as my cornerstone means my foundations for life are in His life that lives in me. It means I trust in the Lord deeply, from the heart, believing He holds everything together when I feel like it's falling apart. It means that I choose to go on living in step with Him as He leads my life, with the result that people can see His footprints in the ways I choose to live.

Galatians 5:24, 25 *"Those who belong to Christ Jesus have crucified the sinful nature with its passions and desires. Since we live by the Spirit, let us keep in step with the Spirit."*

He Must Increase; I Must Decrease

John 3:30 *"He must become greater; I must become less."*

Far too many of us who name His Name as Savior and Lord have it right in our heads, that is we think the right kinds of thoughts, and pray, "My life is yours and I'm about the glory of your Name on earth." But then when it comes time to live what we have said we believe, in times of suffering when life hurts and you don't know what to do, we tend to fret and fuss to one another as though it all depends on our ability to handle it and fix it all.

John the Baptist really had it right. John has the heart part absolutely nailed! These words flowing from his heart of love for Christ and the glory of Jesus on the earth are powerful and timeless. I'm the friend of the bridegroom. My joy is complete and absolute right now because I have heard the shout and have seen his joy.

This is the secret to a life of fruitfulness in the kingdom of God for every person who has believed and received Jesus as Savior and Lord. He must become greater in my life and my puny ability to do anything meaningful for God must become less in my own eyes. Knowing Jesus personally and deeply, His heart living in my heart, His will impassioning my actions, this is the central issue of a fruitful life in His kingdom of the heart.

John the Baptist articulates the thought about how to live a fruitful life in God's kingdom this way, in John 3:27, *"A man can receive only what is given him from heaven."*

Dr Gene Peterson in the MESSAGE states these it in this way: *"It is not possible for a person to succeed – I'm talking about eternal success – without heaven's help."*

Jesus said it this way in John 15:5 *I am the vine; you are the branches. If a man remains in me and I in him, he will bear much fruit; apart from me you can do nothing."*

Building my life on Jesus the precious cornerstone means that my life is not my own, and that I am constrained in heart by a love that is larger than my self-interest, my plans and my will for my life.

II Corinthians 5:14, 15 *"For Christ's love compels us, because we are convinced that one died for all, and therefore all died. And he died for all, that those who live should no longer live for themselves but for him who died for them and was raised again."*

You may be asking yourself the key question of life right now. How do I do this? How does He increase and how do I become less in my own life every day? The answer is simple but yet it is extremely difficult to do. Fall on the cornerstone and be broken in heart each new day. It cuts at everything the world system I live in tells me is important. The way of the world is to watch out for ol' number one, to make your own way.

The way of the kingdom is the path of voluntary humility and embracing what Jesus has done for me. The way for me to choose to live with more of Jesus' life living in my life and less of me is to embrace the way of the cross. The truth is that the life of Jesus is only free to rule at the places of the heart where we are dead to sin and self-interest.

Galatians 2:20 *"I have been crucified with Christ and I no longer live, but Christ lives in me. The life I live in the body, I live by faith in the Son of God, who loved me and gave himself for me."*

Galatians 5:24, 25 *"Those who belong to Christ Jesus have crucified the sinful nature with its passions and desires. Since we live by the Spirit, let us keep in step with the Spirit."*

My Hegai questions for you are really simple: What are you building in your life? What foundation are you building it on? Whose Christian life is richer and better because you are in it with them encouraging them?

A life that really matters is one that is invested in things that are out of this world in terms of their value. You and I have the incredible privilege of choosing the things that delight the king. So let's get on with throwing ourselves into His delights with every ounce of spiritual passion we can muster!

Chapter Thirteen

Integrity of Heart

One last time, let's remember our crucial question we are asking together as the foundation of our study. What does our Lord delight in, esteem as precious, of inestimable valuable? The reason for asking that question is simple. If we understand from God's revealed Word what He holds as precious and we are His royal subjects we will know what we are called to value in our hearts. And further, if we know what is precious to God we will also have a fundamental understanding of things we can do to please Him, make our King's heart rejoice, and bring Him great delight!

We've also noted a rather basic understanding of what it means to be the people of God, members of His Kingdom here on earth. We have been made part of His holy kingdom of the heart, which places us squarely in opposition to the attitudes, ways, and values of this world system we live in. The Scriptures talk about our "not loving the world" – meaning the system of life you find yourself in that is a combination of the thinking of sinful, the depraved thinking of people, and the wiles of Satan who is "prince of this world." The Bible calls us to love God, one another as Christians, and the lost people of our created world. And it calls us to reject loving or embracing the world system or cultural values.

John 14:18, 19 Jesus said, *"If the world hates you, keep in mind that it hated me first. If you belonged to the world it would love you as its own. As it is, you do not belong to the world, but I have chosen you out of the world. That is why the world hates you."*

I John 2:15 – 17 John taught us as adherents to Jesus' Kingdom here on earth: *"Do not love the world. If anyone loves the world, the love of the Father is not in him. For everything in the world – the cravings of sinful man, the lust of his eyes and the boasting of what he has and does – comes not from the Father but from the world. The world and its desires pass away, but the man who does the will of God lives forever."*

As followers of Jesus Christ, we must make decisions on an ongoing basis to embrace the values of His kingdom, God's good, pleasing, and perfect will, and to reject the values of our world system. This system plays to our sinful, fleshly nature to entice us to turn away from God's ways. We must realize this warfare of values we are in and be willing to pass our attitudes, actions, and lifestyle under the scrutiny of the question, "am I embracing what is precious to you here Father God? Am I embracing your Kingdom values here or the ways of my world culture?"

The people of God in Christ Jesus who are walking in the light of His Kingdom values here on planet earth have chosen to take into consideration that we are living a counter-culture lifestyle. Further, we are learning what it means to pray in the garden of our own souls with Jesus – "it doesn't matter to me Father what I want here, as much as it matters to me what you want here." *"Not my will but your will be done, Father."*

As we begin this chapter we are looking at our last picture of embracing what God delights in and highly esteems: Being people who cherish truth in our inmost being, being people of integrity. It is really important that we begin with a definition of this often-used, yet perhaps not clearly understood, word. Integrity, according to Webster's Dictionary, is defined as "wholeness, probity, moral soundness, the quality or state of being unimpaired." In more practical terms, integrity can be thought of as "being on the inside what we appear to be on the outside." It is to actually be, in terms of character and quality of life, what we say we are. One of my favorite ways to think of integrity is the nautical sense of the term. A ship is said to have integrity when it can remain afloat on the high seas, or the storms of life.

The Scriptures show us how God feels about people of integrity. In the midst of a heartrending song or repentance David wrote in Psalm 51:5, 6, *"Surely I was sinful at birth, sinful from the time my mother conceived me. Surely you desire truth in the inner parts; you teach me wisdom in the inmost place."*

Proverbs 11:1 *"The Lord hates cheating, but he delights in honesty."*

Proverbs 11:20 *"The Lord hates people with twisted hearts, but he delights in those who have integrity."*

God takes great delight in integrity in His sons and daughter's lives. Integrity is to be on the inside what we say we are on the outside. It is to be able to stay afloat when we're on the high seas and things get stormy. Integrity demands that we be people who walk in truth in our inmost being, a heart that longs to do the right thing to honor the King.

Thomas A'Kempis wrote the following quote in "The Imitation of Christ." "The more a man is united within himself, and becometh inwardly simple, so much the more and higher things doth he understand without labor; for that he receiveth intellectual light from above. A pure, sincere, and stable spirit is not distracted though it be employed in many works; because it works all to the honor of God, and inwardly being still and quiet, seeks not itself in anything it doth. Who hinders and troubles thee more than the unmortified affections of thine own heart?" That'll work in one's heart, won't it?

As one analyzes Jesus' teaching and the teaching of those who wrote of Him in Scripture, integrity is really wholeness, soundness, which resides first in the heart and then works its way out to the outer world. Consider the clear teaching of Scripture with me as we unpack what integrity is and does. Jesus was speaking to a teacher of the law about loving God supremely and your neighbor as yourself. In that context He spoke about experiencing and expressing love for God from the inside out, with every part and fiber of our being. Notice with me the incredible picture of integrity this is. Jesus clearly told us where loving service springs from first: It's the heart and then it proceeds outward to the soul, the mind, and ultimately affects the actions.

Mark 12:30 *"Love the Lord your God with all your heart and with all your soul and with all your mind and with all your strength."*

In His Sermon on the Mount, Matthew 5, 6, and 7, Jesus began with God-honoring attitudes, then went to God-honoring relationships with others and then proceeded to God-honoring actions in the ways that we choose to live with others. His concept of integrity is clearly in focus as an outline to that powerful passage of Scripture.

The Apostle Paul didn't miss this heavenly mandate of Jesus regarding what integrity is and does as it walks through life as a member of His kingdom of the heart. In writing to the Thessalonians Paul spoke to them about soundness, integrity, holiness encompassing the whole person.

I Thessalonians 5:23, 24 *"May God himself, the God of peace, sanctify you through and through. May your whole spirit, soul, and body be kept blameless at the coming of our Lord Jesus Christ. The one who calls you is faithful and he will do it."*

Integrity is wholeness and soundness that affects the whole life from the inside out. It demands a deepening of our relationships with others in our lives. This is true for all of those who would know and walk with God in everyday life. Paul wrote about this in giving counsel to his two sons in the faith, Timothy and Titus. He counseled them to look at the primacy of integrity in relationships, when they worked to place people in spiritual leadership in the infant churches they had planted together.

Notice the various areas Paul wrote to Timothy and Titus regarding what to look for in terms of integrity in the lives of people. He taught them to look at significant relationships in the following categories.

Integrity in Marriage and Family

Without question the first place a believer demonstrates integrity is in the confines of his own home. Whether or not one is a person of integrity will be clearly demonstrated in their marriage and family relationships. Paul's counsel to his young pastor friends is clear in this area.

I Timothy 3:2, 4 and 5 *"Now an overseer must be above reproach, the husband of but one wife, temperate, self-controlled, respectable, hospitable, able to teach, . . . He must manage his own family well and see that his children obey him with proper respect. (If anyone does not know how to manage his own family, how can he take care of God's church?)*

Titus 1:6, 7a *"An elder must be blameless, the husband of but one wife, a man whose children believe and are not open to the charge of being wild and disobedient. Since an overseer is entrusted with God's work he must be blameless – not overbearing, not quick tempered, . . ."*

This isn't rocket science is it? Paul was telling these young pastors that the marriage and family life of a perspective leadership person is the first thing to look at to decide how well the person is living a life of integrity. Being able to love, care for, submit to, and serve one mate for a lifetime is a pretty valuable picture of integrity of heart. A believer who is a person of integrity will be able to function well in the local body of believers in partnership with his/her spouse. Their marital relationship will be foundational to other wonderfully solid relationships in the local body of believers.

What was true then is still true today. If a person cannot dwell in deepening levels of intimate relationship with their spouse, they most probably will not develop quality relationships with their children. If they lack integrity in their home life, they most definitely will not be able to lead well in the life of the church.

Integrity demands that we be people who interact with others in the local church on the basis of a solid marriage and mutual love and respect dwelling in our significant relationships. Speaking from the heart, I have had more than my share of experiences with people who have had unhealthy relationships in their marriage or family. It affects every other area of their lives.

Essentially what very often happens is that people who struggle with intimacy in their relationships will mask this by getting involved in lots of activities. Doing lots of good things cannot take the place of being able to get along well with people. Eventually lack of intimacy with significant people in a person's life will be evident to everyone because when one is lacking in people skills, it will show up first in their family relationships. The world of that "believer" will come crashing down, along with lots of people whom they have influenced.

Do you want to know how well a person is doing in the issue of integrity in their home-life? Look at the countenance of their spouse and children, in an unguarded moment, when the prospective leader is giving testimony or doing some type of ministry. They will either affirm or their countenance will be reflecting a "yeah, right" perspective.

Integrity with the Next Generation of Christians

II Timothy 2:1, 2 *"You then, my son, be strong in the grace that is in Christ Jesus. And the things you have heard me say in the presence of many witnesses entrust to reliable men who will be qualified to teach others."*

Matthew 10 is a chapter containing what Jesus told His disciples when He sent them out to preach the Good News of the Kingdom. There are two phrases I want to pull out of that teaching session, which from my perspective, get at the principle of integrity with the next generation of Christians. Jesus commands His followers of all time to give to others what has been entrusted to us. Look at His clearly spoken words in verse 8a, *"Freely you have received, freely give."* Again in verse 27 *"What I tell you in the dark, speak in the daylight; what is whispered in your ear, proclaim from the roofs."*

Believers who clearly understand the ethics and the principles of the Kingdom of God know that what we have been given we are entrusted with giving to others. This includes our correctly handling the deep truths of the faith and longing to pass them along to those who are younger than we are. In the kingdom of God, what we give we truly possess and what we keep we lose. Picture it like trying to hold a handful of Jell-O. The tighter you hold it the less you have!

This is how it is in the Kingdom of God on the earth. Paul's word to Timothy was really clear. What Timothy had received from the Lord through Paul's life he was responsible to give to others who would in turn give it to others! Show me a person who doesn't care about those younger in the faith, with potential to be awesome followers of Jesus, and I'll show you a person who doesn't understand the Kingdom of God.

The next generation of followers of Jesus, members of this incredible Kingdom of God, won't evolve from good intentions. They won't spontaneously arise from good churches with good preaching and teaching systems. They must be identified, encouraged, and invested in with care and consistency. They will need a carefully constructed environment of discipleship, which gives them a place to learn that is safe. True believers care more about the Kingdom than they do about anything else in life. These believers give to others who are younger in the faith, what we have been so freely given.

Integrity with the Local Body of Believers

I Timothy 3:6 *"He must not be a recent convert, or he may become conceited and fall under the same judgment as the devil."*

Titus 1:9 *"He must hold firmly to the trustworthy message as it has been taught, so he can encourage others by sound doctrine and refute those who oppose it."*

Regarding Deacons Paul wrote, I Timothy 3:9, 10 *"They must keep hold of the deep truths of the faith with a clear conscience. They must first be tested; and then if there is nothing against them, let them serve as deacons."*

Paul's words to his young pastor brothers, Timothy and Titus, are clear and to the point. The third place we carefully attend to integrity in our own lives, and in the lives of others, is in the relationships they have developed in the local body. This integrity issue gets at the questions regarding how well a person "wears" as people "try on" relationships with them.

Since the Kingdom of God is wholly about people, it is vital that we pay attention to the trail we are leaving behind us in the family of believers. All of us cut a wake in the lives of other people, in the same way that a huge ship leaves a wake in the water. The fruit of what we have meant to people and how we have related to them is left in their lives. Jesus said, *"By their fruit you will recognize them,"* in Matthew 7:16.

It is crucial that people who have been called to Kingdom living do so from the foundation stone of solid relationships in their local church. This is the place where ministry callings and gifts are first heard and developed in a person's life. Therefore, it is the first public place of affirmation regarding what we sense God is saying about His future for us in ministry opportunities. Kingdom minded people, who want to develop others for future ministry roles will find places for them to serve in the local church. They will invest in them by giving them ministry opportunities in their local church. The goal is to allow them to employ their gifts and callings in the local church to test them in an environment of growth and development in which it is safe to make mistakes.

Paul's counsel to Timothy regarding his placing people in the role of diaconate in the local church was that they should first be tested. Don't put recent converts into key leadership positions, lest they get filled with pride. Let them first be tested in other areas of service. Then, when we see what fruit they are leaving behind them in the lives of others, they can be given more significant leadership roles.

Integrity with the Unchurched and Prechristian World

The fourth and final place we must view through the lenses of leading a life of of integrity is in the relationships we have with people who aren't yet the children of God in Christ Jesus. I Timothy 3:7 *"He must also have a good reputation with outsiders, so that he will not fall into disgrace and into the devil's trap."* There are two ways to look at what Paul is saying here. The first is to see the words *"reputation with outsiders"* as solely those outside the church relationship circles. In that case Paul was telling the reader to see to it that our relationships in the business world, the practical elements of life, are in order. We pay our bills on time, we beat no one out of what we owe them, and we file honest tax returns. But there's a better way to view this verse and that is to see the outsiders as those who are outside the kingdom of God. In this viewpoint we pay careful attention to how well we treat these people, who are often referred to in church circles as "sinners."

How deeply we care about unchurched and prechristian people is perhaps the greatest measuring tool we have to know, in reality, how much of God's heart beats in our hearts. Sinners, which all of us were at one time, are why Jesus became a human being. He became one of us so that He would have blood to shed. He shed His blood for us because it was the only redemption price the Father God would accept for us. The tremendous love and mercy of God for us is what caused Jesus to come to rescue us.

Jesus gave us His statement of purpose in Luke 19:10 *"The Son of man came to seek and to save what was lost."* At the very minimum, we must pray for them, love them, and care deeply for them because God loves them so much. If we know and love God at deepening levels of intimacy, He will be imparting more and more of His heart to us. His heart of love and mercy, compassion and grace for the lost will live in us, moving us to invest in these relationships as true friends.

When my wife and I were far from God, we often spent Friday evenings with my uncle Sam Hepner and my grandma Sally Hepner, sitting in their home with them. We were sinners, who were essentially completely unchurched. We didn't look, act, or smell like Christians in any way, shape, or form. They were members of a conservative Mennonite church in Juniata County, Pennsylvania. They simply loved us and cared about our lost hearts and souls. Friday night after Friday night they loved us and visited with us, and often explained to us the way of salvation. My uncle Sam told us about Jesus and my Grandma sat there silently praying for us as two hungry hearts listened. What I would later come to learn was that my Grandma had been praying for me to know her Savior Jesus, three times a day for 22 years! I wonder why I was drawn to her home to find Christ?

One Saturday morning the message I had been hearing for many months clicked in my heart. The Holy Spirit's conviction broke me and I gave my heart to the Lord in a front-end loader in a limestone quarry.

I was radically and permanently changed because two people loved on Raina and me and showed us who Jesus is, what He came to do for us, and made it personal for us so we could understand. I want to invest the rest of my life in doing what they did for me.

Well, this is your friend Hegai speaking again – there you have them. Four areas to look at our own lives in terms of the integrity. Then we take the same lenses of integrity in these four areas and look at the lives of others in our sphere of influence. The goal is to walk with Jesus and in relationships with other believers from the solid foundation stone of integrity in our marriage and family, with the next generation of believers, with the local body, and with the unchurched and prechristians in our spheres of influence. The people in whom we will seek to invest the kingdom will sometimes be pretty rough around the edges in some of these areas. I know I certainly was. But the real issue we want to see in others is deep heart hunger to know the King more intimately. God works with hungry hearts. We can too!

Chapter Fourteen

"Yoked to His Heart"

As I began this book I invited you to join me in a journey of the heart. There were a number of things I shared with you that I think are absolutely profound and bear repeating before we get into the thing I want to leave you with. We are all involved in a battle for the contents, character, and affections of our hearts! We are all involved in the daily battle to make quality choices of the heart, to espouse godly desires within, and then act in our lifestyle choices in God-honoring ways.

You and I are in a significant battle for the contents of our hearts and our choices in matters of the heart are paramount to a God-honoring and Jesus-glorifying life. The Lord desires that we embrace a childlike, broken, contrite heart of surrender to His will and purposes for life. The enemy wants to defile our hearts, causing us to go after selfish choices and the ways of this world system of things. The following Scriptures are foundational to understanding the integral nature of this "heart battle."

Proverbs 4:23 *"Above all else guard your heart for it is the wellspring of life."*

Paul prayed for the Ephesian believers to experience the indwelling Holy Spirit in their hearts: *"I pray that out of his glorious riches he may strengthen you with power through his Spirit in your inner being, so that Christ may dwell in your hearts through faith."* Ephesians 3:16, 17a

Romans 5:5 *"And hope does not disappoint us, because God has poured out his love into our hearts by the Holy Spirit, whom he has given us."*

Our part in this process of knowing and walking with God in deepening, intimate relationship is to cultivate a soft and teachable heart, a childlike trust and surrender of our will, plans, and purposes, to His heart's desires. The truth is that this King, who has loved us with an everlasting love, actually wants to be intimately involved in our everyday lives. He actually wants to meet with us in the morning and invites us to "tie in" to His heart's desires.

May I be straight with you? I'm going to be, but I thought I should at least ask for your permission. It seems to me that one of the big problems we face in the church inNorth America is pride in how wise we are, pride in our ability to know and interpret the Bible. We seem to take great pride in intellect and in educational pursuits, as though somehow, these intellectual disciplines will make us more like Jesus.

Do you remember what Jesus said about the kind of person He delights in? *"He called a little child and had him stand among them. And he said, 'I tell you the truth, unless you change and become like little children, you will never enter the kingdom of heaven. Therefore, whoever humbles himself like this child is the greatest in the kingdom of heaven."*

Do you ever think of yourself as a small child? Jesus seemed to think that was an important attitude to cultivate so I think it's a good question. A little child knows himself to be small, knows he doesn't know everything but his daddy does, and isn't shy about asking questions. This is something the Father God seems to take great delight in, because He gave us all a clear mandate to embrace this attitude through the words of Jesus. The essence of kingdom entry and maturity is a humble and childlike heart attitude!

In this last chapter of this work, our theme is the essence of what it means to seek to live a Christian life. The Lord has impressed this deeply in my heart and my desire is to invest the rest of my life learning what this means. ***The essence of the Christian life is the forming of the life of Jesus Christ in you and me, by the powerful presence of the Holy Spirit living in us!***

Our goal is to live a Christ-like life. We are not going to be able to accomplish this in our human strength, nor will we be able to do so with our best grit, will, or determination. To believe I can live a Christian life on my own disciplines alone is essentially to take pride in my ability to do things for God. That kind of approach is destined to leave us tired, defeated, and disillusioned.

To accomplish my goal of Christ-like living requires that I reject the temptation to think that I can do it. It is to humbly come to the cross of Jesus each new day, and choose to live, *"crucified with Christ, nevertheless I live, yet not I but Christ lives in me."*

The Lord Jesus was the only person who ever lived a life that was perfectly pleasing to the Father God in every way. He is the only person who could ever say, *"the prince of this world has no hold on me."* (See John 14:30) He taught His followers how we could walk a victorious Christian life, Luke 9:23, 24. *"If anyone would come after me, he must deny himself, take up his cross daily, and follow me. For whoever wants to save his life will lose it, but whoever loses his life for me will save it."*

The principle we are building on is this: ***Jesus is divine life lived in the human arena.*** As we believe in Him and receive Him in our hearts and lives by faith, He dwells in us by His Holy Spirit and the Spirit makes Jesus' life a reality in our lives. There are two of us living in here.

John 14:6 *"I am the way and the truth and the life. No one comes to the Father except through me."*

I John 5:12 *"He who has the Son has life; he who does not have the Son of God does not have life."*

Romans 8:9 *"And if anyone does not have the Spirit of Christ he does not belong to Christ."*

Our foundational building block is profound yet so simple: ***Our goal is to be Christ-like and only Jesus can be Jesus in me!*** You and I have the incredible privilege of having the Spirit of God dwelling in our lives, making our Spirit-person, which was dead in transgressions and sins, to become alive in Christ Jesus our Lord. As He dwells in our hearts and lives He makes Jesus' life a present reality.

Galatians 5:24, 25 *"Those who belong to Christ Jesus have crucified the sinful nature with its passions and desires. Since we live by the Spirit, let us keep in step with the Spirit."*

There is a companion principle we must be gripped by if we are to mature in our understanding of what it means to be His disciples. **The second principle** is one that we have already studied in this book: ***Life through death.*** It is only as we choose to go by faith to the cross of Jesus each day and live crucified with Him to our humanity, the fleshly nature, and the allure of this world that He pours His life into our lives.

The resurrection power of God to live above sin and this world is only poured into those who choose to live dead to sin, self-interest, and this world order of things in Christ Jesus, by faith. Resurrections only occur in cemeteries.

II Corinthians 4:11 *"For we who are alive are always being given over to death for Jesus' sake, so that His life may be revealed in our mortal body."*

I'm back to my original point of origin, regarding the essence of the Christian life. It is the person of Jesus Christ living in me by His Spirit. Paul wrote to the Galatian believers, 4:19 *"My dear children for whom I am again in the pains of childbirth, until Christ is formed in you."*

The essence of Christian discipleship is to be with Jesus. The essence of maturation as His followers is to live with less of me and more of Him living in my life. This is accomplished by going to the cross by faith each day taking His provisions into my life by faith.

To make this understanding of the Christian life live just a little more for us, let's turn our attention to a marvelous word picture in Scripture, which Jesus gave to His followers in Matthew 11:28 – 30. *"Come to me all you who are weary and burdened and I will give you rest. Take my yoke upon you and learn of me, for I am gentle and humble in heart and you will find rest for your souls. For my yoke is easy and my burden is light."*

The Powerful Word Picture:

I don't think I ever really understood this word picture at all, until God permitted me to preach at a pastor's training school near Madras in India. It was in 1995 when the Lord gave me my first truly cross-cultural preaching experience of my life. There, in Madras in southern India, I saw ox-carts as one of their chief means of plowing, harvesting, and getting their produce to market, very similarly to the way things were in Jesus day.

Being the classic North American believer, I always had seen this as a one-ox yoke. What that gave me was a perspective that I was responsible to put His yoke on me and pull the weight He had permitted to be brought into my life and ministry. But what I saw in Southern India challenged my ways to the core of my being. I was there to help the students in the pastor training school, but God used my experience there to shape my heart for the rest of my days as His man. I spent a great deal of time alone on the floor of my dorm room repenting of my self-focused and self-centered thinking.

Jesus was giving us a picture of His deep desire to walk with us through life, to do works with us, together in fellowship every day. His word picture is that of a two-ox-yoke, that was very common in His day. A two-ox-yoke was where a young ox was yoked to a seasoned older ox that had learned how to work in the hot sun all day, how to pace itself at the pace of the driver. I didn't understand this until I saw it in India. I asked the driver of one of the carts why they put a big ox in a yoke with a little ox.

His answer was profound: "Big ox there to pull load. Little ox there to learn how."

The LEAD OX was bigger, stronger, more powerful, mature worker who was one with the driver.

The LITTLE OX was there to learn from the big ox and to become a seasoned worker, as much as, to pull the load.

Listen carefully to the words of Jesus in Matthew 11:29 *"Take my yoke upon you and learn of me."* He is telling us He wants to be in the yoke of life with us, that we may walk together with Him. He is the big ox in my yoke and I am the young ox, and I am walking with Him to learn His ways, His will and desires.

What do we know about young oxen? They can do it, they are tough and strong, they can show people how to do it! They come out and chafe and tug and pull and strain. The big ox just stands there … "When you're through I will show you how to do this, sonny!" Can you relate with me at all to getting tired because deep down in your heart you are attempting to pull the Big Ox through life in doing for Him?

There is a powerful spiritual lesson here for us if we have eyes to see it. Jesus Christ our Lord is in the yoke of life with us as the LEAD OX and we are there with Him as the LITTLE OX. As believers our job is not to chafe, tug, pull, and strain at the load, as though we are attempting to pull the Son of God along through life. I am yoked to Him so that I might learn to walk as He walks, love as He loves, and move at the pace He is leading me.

As the young ox was there to learn from the big ox, I am to put my eyes on Jesus. That is what He meant when He said, *"Take my yoke upon you and learn of me."* It's also what Paul meant when he said, *"Since we live by the Spirit, let us keep in step with the Spirit."*

SOME YOKES THAT MUST BE BROKEN

Matthew 11:29 *"Take my yoke upon you . . . ."*

Please notice with me that being a believer in Christ Jesus requires that we be a one-yoke-person. The yoke of Christ Jesus, being yoked together with Him, is perfectly crafted to fit my shoulders – and therefore it will not fit over another yoke I may be wearing.

Remember in His human trade Jesus was a carpenter, and one of the things carpenters made were wooden yokes, carefully fitted to the shoulders of an ox. Consequently Jesus knows how to craft a wooden yoke to fit our shoulders. If I try to put on His yoke and I have other yokes on me, His yoke will not fit and I am probably going to have sore shoulders.

Consequently, I am responsible to remove any other yokes I may be wearing, being tied to things which may be offending God.

I am responsible to remove the yoke of my will and desires, tying myself down to the things I want, my ways, and my ambitions. The only way I know to destroy the power of my will and ways is to choose to live crucified to my will and desires, putting them to death with Jesus my Lord. I am responsible to embrace His will and desires each new day, embrace His life living in my life.

I am responsible to remove and smash the yoke of sin – the willful breaking of God's desires for my life. We must remove and smash, deal a deathblow to the part of our humanity that leans toward sinning. The prophet Jeremiah wrote to us a clear word about sin being a yoke that can and does sap our strength:

Lamentations 1:14 *"My sins have been bound into a yoke; by his hands they were woven together. They have come upon my neck and the Lord has sapped my strength. He has handed me over to those I cannot withstand."*

Sin can become a binding, a yoke that can lead my life, instead of my desires for righteousness leading my life. Let's be really straight with one another regarding sin. There is only one way to deal with sin over which I am not winning:

Romans 6:11-14 *"count yourselves dead to sin but alive unto God in Christ Jesus. Therefore, do not let sin reign in your mortal body so that you obey its evil desires. Do not offer the parts of your body to sin as instruments of wickedness, but offer yourselves to God, as those who have been brought from death to life; and offer the parts of your body to Him as instruments of righteousness. For sin shall not be your Master, ..."*

WE MUST BE RUTHLESS WITH SIN OR SIN WILL BE RUTHLESS WITH US!

I am responsible to remove and smash being unequally yoked to the world system around me. I cannot love this world, or the things that are in this world and give my primary love to God. The ways of this world are the exact opposite of God's ways. Paul wrote to the Galatians 6:14

"May I never boast except in the cross of our Lord Jesus Christ, through which the world has been crucified to me, and I to the world."

Romans 12:1,2 in the context of offering ourselves to God as living sacrifices Paul wrote, *"do not go steady with the world."* (JBP)

I am responsible to remove and smash the yoke of oppression, which the enemy specializes in bringing against me. The enemy's beings attack us with hopelessness and despair, when we are walking through God's appointed seasons of testing, difficult days. Oppression can be referred to as "the dark night of the soul," which can and does enslave us to fear, to sins, and bondage. Oppression is a weapon of the enemy that seems to have been unleashed at some of God's most choice servants. Remember, it is an "outside-in" tool of the enemy, and it has no power over us unless we permit it to do so.

We do not have to "put up with" or "learn to live with" inner hopelessness or despair or fear. Jesus died for us, shed His blood for us to cancel all the power of the devil. We are responsible to renounce and turn away from oppression and to defeat it through the precious provisions of our Lord Jesus Christ!

II Timothy 1:7 *"For God did not give us a spirit of timidity (fear) but a spirit of power, of love and of self-discipline."*

LEARNING TO BE YOKED TOGETHER WITH JESUS

What we must understand is that Jesus came here and lived among us as a human being. He subjected Himself to temptation, heartache, and suffering. He is the one who is saying to us – "You can't do this without me. You need me to enable you to live victoriously in your every day life!"

He is in essence calling us to make a deliberate choice and calling each of us to take action that must be taken every day. Instead of getting up in the morning and deciding to do my very best to be Christ-life today, to decide to do my best to please Him, there is a better way. I choose to put my shoulders in the two-ox-yoke with my Lord Jesus – my LEAD OX, deliberately looking at Him, and not the task before me!

My task is to do what Jesus did – He went to His Father first, then He set out to do what He heard His Father saying.

John 4:34 *"My food is to do the will of Him who sent me and to finish His work."*

John 5:19 *". . . .the Son can do only what He sees the Father doing."*

John 5:36 *"For the very work the Father has given me to finish, and which I am doing, testifies that the Father has sent me."*

John 8:26 *". . . . what I have heard from Him I tell the world."*

John 8:28 *". . . . I do nothing on my own but speak just what the Father has taught me."*

Here's the Christian life principle, brothers and sisters: My task is to do what Jesus did with the Father if I really want to cooperate with the Father's missionary heart to publish abroad the glory of His Son Jesus!

I am called, by this Biblical picture to *"keep in step with the Spirit"* by getting up in the morning and choosing to simply be with Jesus! I place myself, voluntarily through brokenness and submission into the yoke with Jesus so that the two of us may walk through my life's experiences together today! I don't get up and chafe and strain to act. I get up and submit my will to His will, my heart to His heart. I choose to get into the yoke and look to the right to see what the Big Ox is doing, and then I join Him in His walk through my life.

Charles Blair was a pastor who went to jail for selling bonds that were illegal. He wrote a book that touched my heart: "The Man Who Could

Do No Wrong." There is a quote in that book that is worth the price of the book. "It isn't the tasks before me that dictate what I should do. It is God's particular will for my life that dictates what I should do." My primary task is not to pull the load of ministry for God. It is to fix my eyes on Jesus my King, who has authored a good, pleasing, and perfect will for my life!

The awesome thing for me to consider is that Jesus, my King and Master wants to be yoked together with me! And I am amazed that the awesome Son of God desires to teach me His pace as we walk together through life!

THE LORD'S HEART FOR US AS ADOPTED SONS AND DAUGHTERS

Matthew 11:29b *"learn from me for I am gentle and humble in heart and you will find rest for your souls."*

Our Master never ever left people in doubt to quandary to know what was really in His heart for them. He opened Himself in mercy, compassion and walked among humankind as a person of both love and truth; integrity. In this word picture of being yoked to Him as our Lord Ox in the ox-cart He wants us to see and understand His pace is gentle. His will is to be walked with Him at His pace!

His yoke in His strength is a picture of walking with Him in the center of His will for my life. He wants us to be very clear that His yoke is easier and lighter than human-works yokes; bondage to the tyranny of the here and now, the demands of people, career or lifestyle: Carrying my own load.

He is trying to help us see that His burdens are walked in His strength and His power by His Holy Spirit, not by our best efforts and born on our shoulders alone. In this cultural model of doing activities in the performance treadmill we often bear enormous stress, weight, and are often weary, even though we claim to be His children.

As God's children, who are learning to walk in His model of doing He has some considerable training to do to us. We often spend time asking God what is on His heart and once we hear His whisper we run off and try to do it in our strength like the super-hero. The only time we come back to time with God is when we are in trouble, it is not going well, we are tired and want to quit!

God's purpose in allowing us the incredible privilege of knowing His heart, love, compassion; His burdens is so that we will learn to walk with Him 24 hours a day in the yoke as He bears the weight and pace of the working. He can do His work without us. He wants to partner with us so we can do things together!

Listen to God's response to His special, adopted son Ephraim – Jeremiah 31:20 which, please remember we are using analogously for His special firstborn, adopted sons and daughters in this room today. God doesn't want us to listen long enough to be able to run out of the throne room and do acts for Him. He wants us to walk in His yoke with Him for the rest of our lives. He wants us to bear the fruit He produces: God speaks . . . . .

"Is not Ephraim my dear son, the child in whom I delight? Though I often speak against him, I still remember him. Therefore my heart yearns for him; I have great compassion for him, declares the Lord."

Why had God spoken against Ephraim his special, adopted son? Because he was out there doing wrongly, then doing God's activities and thinking he was OK. Ephraim as a community was on the performance treadmill –all doing and no heart!

But listen to what God really wanted; *"My heart yearns for him."* God didn't want His best efforts, He wanted to dwell with him, be loved by

Him, and to receive His worship. *"My heart yearns for him." "I have great compassion for Him."* Do you identify at all with Ephraim – doing much for God but not walking by faith with him, with lots of dos and don'ts, longing to know God better than we do? Look at the truth of this great text: God's heart yearns for you. God wants to know and be known by you. He's not all that interested in your best efforts to do for him!

Son-daughter – Ephraim, adopted firstborn, chosen and special are you tired of trying to do all you think God wants you to do? Is the pace of life wearing you down? Is it possible that you are in a one-ox-yoke of performance?

OK, just one more time, this is your Hegai speaking. Perhaps the best thing you could do for the next year – for the next 365 days of your life – is join Esther in the decision she made, which won the king's heart. She found someone who knew the king better than she did and learned from him. She immersed herself in what the king liked to eat, smell, taste, and touch. And as a result she and the king enjoyed tremendous intimacy in life. In this book you hold in your hands, I have attempted to do for you what Hegai did for Esther. The King of kings, Jesus wants to be yoked to you. He wants to enjoy your company and walk through your life with you.

Listen closely. I can hear Him whisper to you; *"My heart yearns for you!"*